Weaving Lives
The Essence of Human Connection

Naresh Chandra Nayak

BLUEROSE PUBLISHERS
India | U.K.

Copyright © Naresh Chandra Nayak 2024

All rights reserved by author. No part of this publication may be reproduced, stored in a retrieval system or transmitted in any form or by any means, electronic, mechanical, photocopying, recording or otherwise, without the prior permission of the author. Although every precaution has been taken to verify the accuracy of the information contained herein, the publisher assumes no responsibility for any errors or omissions. No liability is assumed for damages that may result from the use of information contained within.

BlueRose Publishers takes no responsibility for any damages, losses, or liabilities that may arise from the use or misuse of the information, products, or services provided in this publication.

For permissions requests or inquiries regarding this publication, please contact:

BLUEROSE PUBLISHERS
www.BlueRoseONE.com
info@bluerosepublishers.com
+91 8882 898 898
+4407342408967

ISBN: 978-93-6452-677-7

Cover design: Shivani
Typesetting: Rohit

First Edition: September 2024

DEDICATED TO...

To my mother, **Late Elizabeth Nayak**, whose life of care and dedication taught me to fight against the odds. To my **father**, who instilled in me the importance of weaving lives together with patience, persistence, and endurance. And to siblings **Mini, Kuni, Tuna, Tuni, Mamata, Kamini,** *family relations and close friends*, who have always stood by me, demonstrating that those who genuinely love never go away; they walk side by side, holding hands together.

Acknowledgments

I am profoundly grateful to Fr. Joseph Thottamkara CM, Fr. Jose Paimpillikunnel CM, Br. Henaro Pradhan CM, Sr. Mamata Nayak SJA, and Sr. Justine Senapati SJA for their unwavering support and guidance throughout this journey. Their wisdom and unwavering encouragement have been invaluable.

To my family members and friends, for their constant love and belief in me have been my anchor. My sincere gratitude to them all for standing by me and for the endless support I experience.

Finally, to the readers of **Weaving Lives**, thank you for taking the time to engage with my work. Your interest, time, and trust are what will make our life journey truly meaningful with genuine connection.

Introduction

In an age where the world seems more connected yet more divided than ever, the wisdom of truly living with and understanding others has never been more essential. "Weaving Lives: The Essence of Human Connection" is a guide to navigating the complexities of human relationships, drawing from timeless principles and contemporary insights to foster deeper connections, empathy, and harmonious coexistence.

This book is not merely about social skills or etiquette; it delves into the essence of what it means to coexist meaningfully with others. It addresses the foundational aspects of human interaction: communication, empathy, respect, and mutual support. By exploring these elements, "Weaving Lives: The Essence of Human Connection" offers readers practical tools and philosophical reflections to enhance their personal and professional lives.

Understanding Human Nature

At its core, "Weaving Lives: The Essence of Human Connection" begins with an exploration of human nature. Understanding what drives people—their fears, desires, strengths, and weaknesses—is the first step towards meaningful relationships. This section draws from psychology, philosophy, and cultural studies to provide a comprehensive understanding of the human condition.

Effective Communication

Communication is the lifeblood of any relationship. This book delves into both verbal and non-verbal communication, offering techniques to improve clarity, active listening, and emotional intelligence. It emphasizes the importance of empathy in communication, ensuring that we not only hear but truly understand and connect with others.

Building Empathy and Compassion

Empathy is the ability to put oneself in another's shoes, to understand and share their feelings. This section provides exercises and reflections to cultivate empathy and compassion. By doing so, it promotes a culture of kindness and understanding, essential for both personal growth and societal harmony.

Conflict Resolution

Conflict is an inevitable part of human interaction. "Weaving Lives: The Essence of Human Connection" equips readers with strategies for resolving disagreements constructively. It emphasizes the importance of addressing issues directly yet compassionately, fostering a spirit of collaboration rather than confrontation.

Cultivating Respect and Mutual Support

Respect is the foundation of any healthy relationship. This book discusses the importance of respecting diverse perspectives and backgrounds. It also highlights the significance of mutual support—how we can uplift and encourage each other in our personal and collective journeys.

Living in Community

Humans are inherently social beings, and living well with others involves creating and nurturing communities. This section explores how to build inclusive, supportive communities that value every individual. It discusses the roles of leadership, shared values, and collective responsibility in fostering a sense of belonging.

Personal Growth and Self-awareness

Finally, "Weaving Lives: The Essence of Human Connection" emphasizes that understanding others begins with understanding oneself. It encourages readers to engage in continuous self-reflection and personal development, recognizing that the journey towards better relationships is also a journey towards better self-awareness and self-improvement.

Conclusion

"Weaving Lives: The Essence of Human Connection" is more than a guidebook; it is a call to action. In its pages, you will find the tools and inspiration to cultivate deeper, more fulfilling relationships. By embracing the principles of empathy, respect, and compassion, we can transform not only our interactions but also our communities and, ultimately, our world.

Contents

1. Inspiring the Youth: A guide to Shaping the Future 1
2. Educate the Future by Educating Children 23
3. Always Help the Elderly 31
4. Inheriting the wisdom of the Ages 39
5. Applauding Leadership Prowess 47
6. Wise to be Away from the Foolish 59
7. Treasuring Humility from the Humble 77
8. Better to Ignore the Arrogants 93
9. Being Closer to the Graceful 105
10. Elevating Aspirational People 113
11. Supporting Strength 122
12. Bless The Godly 130
13. Honoring Wisdom and Experience of the Aged 138
14. Empowering The Vulnerable 145
15. Nurturing Determination and Resilience 152
16. Esteeming Kind People: Honoring Acts of Compassion and Generosity 160
17. Promote The Honest : Elevating Integrity and Trust .. 167

18. Rewarding The Virtuous : Honoring Excellence in Character 174
19. In Weaving Lives : Watch, Pray, and Wish Everyone Well 186

Chapter-1

Inspiring the Youth:

A guide to Shaping the Future

Inspiring young people is not just a noble endeavor; it is a vital investment in our future. When we inspire the youth, we ignite their potential, shape their values, and guide them towards a brighter path. This chapter explores practical strategies and powerful examples to help you inspire the young people you encounter.

A Beacon of Hope: The Story of Anjali

The summer of 2017 was particularly memorable for Father Norbert. As the principal of De Paul Academy, he had seen countless students pass through the hall of fame, each with their own dreams and challenges. However, one student stood out that year a young girl named Anjali. Her story of transformation and inspiration left an indelible mark on the heart of Fater Norbert and reinforced his belief in the power of mentorship.

Anjali came from a modest background. Her father worked as a security guard, and her mother did odd jobs to support the family. Despite their financial struggles, Anjali's parents were determined to give her the best education possible. When Anjali first joined De Paul Academy, she was a shy, reserved girl who often kept to herself. She had potential, but her circumstances had instilled in her a sense of self-doubt.

One day, during a routine school assembly, Father Norbert announced about an upcoming science fair. He noticed Anjali's eyes light up with interest, yet she remained seated, hesitant to participate. After the assembly, Father Norbert approached her and asked if she had any ideas for the fair. Her face lit up as she shyly shared her fascination with renewable energy, a topic she had been reading about at the local library.

Recognizing her enthusiasm, the principal encouraged Anjali to develop a project on solar energy. Over the next few weeks, he spent time mentoring Anjali, providing resources, and connecting her with science teachers who could guide her technical work. Anjali's dedication was inspiring, she spent countless hours researching, experimenting, and perfecting her project.

The day of the science fair arrived, and Anjali's project was nothing short of impressive. She had created a working model of a solar-powered water purification system, designed to provide clean drinking water to rural communities. Her presentation was articulate, and her passion was evident. The judges were amazed, and Anjali won first prize.

The victory was more than just a trophy; it was a turning point in Anjali's life. The recognition boosted her confidence and opened doors to new opportunities. She was invited to participate in regional science competitions, where she continued to excel. Her story caught the attention of local media, and she became a source of inspiration for other students.

Anjali's journey did not stop there. Encouraged by her success, she became an active member of the school's science club, mentoring younger students and sharing her experiences. She even started a community initiative to teach underprivileged children about renewable energy, demonstrating that inspiration can indeed create a ripple effect.

Years later, Anjali graduated with honors and received a scholarship to study environmental engineering at a prestigious university. She kept in touch Father Norbert, and she often reminded him of the impact that one small encouragement had on her life. Today, Anjali is a successful engineer working on sustainable energy projects that benefit communities worldwide.

Life Lessons from Anjali's Story

1. Believe in the Potential of Others:

- Anjali's story underscores the importance of recognizing and nurturing the hidden potential in young individuals. Often, all it takes is someone to believe in them and provide a little encouragement to unlock their capabilities.

2. The Power of Mentorship:

- Effective mentorship can be a game-changer. By guiding Anjali and providing her with the necessary resources and support, the principal was able to help transform her interest into a passion and her passion into a success story. Mentorship is about providing direction, encouragement, and wisdom.

3. Small Acts of Encouragement Make a Big Difference:

- A simple conversation after the school assembly set Anjali on a path of discovery and success. This highlights how small, seemingly insignificant acts of encouragement can have profound impacts on a person's life.

4. Overcoming Self-Doubt:

- Anjali's initial hesitation and self-doubt were significant barriers. Her journey teaches us that overcoming self-doubt is crucial for growth. Support and encouragement from others can help young people build the confidence needed to pursue their dreams.

5. Celebrating Success:

- Recognizing and celebrating achievements, no matter how small, can significantly boost confidence and motivation. Anjali's victory in the science fair was a pivotal moment that validated her hard work and inspired her to aim even higher.

6. The Ripple Effect of Inspiration:

- Inspired by her own journey, Anjali went on to mentor other students and initiate community projects. This demonstrates the ripple effect of inspiration one person's success can inspire many others to pursue their dreams and contribute positively to their communities.

7. Perseverance and Hard Work:

- Anjali's dedication to her project, spending countless hours researching and experimenting, showcases the importance of perseverance and hard work. Success often comes to those who are willing to put in the effort and stay committed to their goals.

8. Giving Back:

- Anjali's initiative to teach underprivileged children about renewable energy illustrates the importance of giving back to the community. Inspiring the youth also means instilling in them a sense of responsibility and the desire to contribute to the greater good.

9. The Importance of Education:

- Anjali's journey from a shy girl to a confident engineer underscores the transformative power of education. Education not only imparts knowledge but also builds confidence, opens doors to opportunities, and shapes future leaders.

10. Legacy of Inspiration:

- By investing time and effort in inspiring the youth, we create a lasting legacy. The impact of such inspiration goes beyond individual success, influencing the broader community and future generations.

These lessons emphasize the importance of believing in and supporting the youth, providing mentorship, celebrating their achievements, and encouraging them to give back. By doing so, we not only help them realize their full potential but also contribute to a better, more inspired world.

Practical Strategies for Inspiring the Youth

The Power of Role Models

"Children have never been very good at listening to their elders, but they have never failed to imitate them."

- James Baldwin

Young people look up to adults as role models. Your actions, words, and attitudes can profoundly influence their lives. To inspire them, embody the qualities you wish to see in them. Be a person of integrity, kindness, and resilience. Demonstrate through your behavior the values and principles you hold dear.

The Story of Malala: A Voice for Education

In the picturesque Swat Valley of Pakistan, a young girl named Malala Yousafzai grew up with dreams as vast as the mountains that surrounded her home. From a tender age, Malala was captivated by the magic of books and the power of knowledge. Her father, Ziauddin Yousafzai, was her greatest inspiration—a passionate educator who believed that every girl had the right to learn.

Ziauddin's unwavering support and bold advocacy for education set the stage for Malala's extraordinary journey. Despite living in a region where the Taliban sought to crush the dreams of girls by banning their education, Malala found her voice. She began to speak out, writing a blog under a pseudonym and giving interviews to raise awareness about the plight of girls in her community.

The world started to listen, but so did the Taliban. On a fateful day in October 2012, their brutal attempt to silence her only amplified her voice. Miraculously surviving a gunshot to the head, Malala's spirit remained unbroken. Her recovery was nothing short of remarkable, and her resolve to fight for education grew even stronger.

Malala's courage resonated globally, turning her into an international symbol of resilience and hope. At just 17, she became the youngest-ever Nobel Peace Prize laureate, standing before world leaders to advocate for the millions of girls deprived of education. Her father, always by her side, continued to be her steadfast supporter and partner in this noble cause.

"**Malala: A Voice for Education**" is an inspiring tale of bravery, the unbreakable bond between a father and daughter, and the relentless pursuit of a world where every child can hold a book and dream freely.

Encouraging Dreams and Aspirations

"Go confidently in the direction of your dreams. Live the life you have imagined."

- Henry David Thoreau

Encourage young people to dream big and pursue their passions. Show interest in their aspirations and provide the guidance and resources they need to achieve them. Help them see that their dreams are attainable with hard work, dedication, and the right support.

Oprah Winfrey's story is one of overcoming adversity. Growing up in poverty, she was inspired by her grandmother's belief in her potential and her father's emphasis on education. These influences encouraged Oprah to pursue her dreams, leading her to become one of the most influential women in the world. Her story is a testament to the power of encouragement and support in helping young people achieve greatness.

Teaching Resilience and Perseverance

"Success is not final, failure is not fatal: It is the courage to continue that counts."

- Winston Churchill

Life is filled with challenges, and young people need to learn resilience and perseverance to navigate them. Share stories of overcoming obstacles and emphasize the importance of persistence. Encourage them to view failures as learning opportunities rather than setbacks.

Arunima Sinha: Conquering Everest

In the bustling city of Lucknow, India, a young woman named Arunima Sinha dreamt of a life filled with sports and adventure. A national-level volleyball player, her aspirations were abruptly shattered in 2011 when she was pushed from a moving train by robbers. The accident resulted in the loss of her left leg, plunging her into a period of darkness and despair.

However, Arunima's indomitable spirit refused to be defeated. During her recovery, she made a bold decision: she would climb Mount Everest. This audacious goal seemed impossible to many, but not to Arunima. With a prosthetic leg and an unyielding determination, she began her training under the guidance of Bachendri Pal, the first Indian woman to summit Everest.

The journey to the top of the world was fraught with immense physical and emotional challenges. Battling extreme weather, treacherous terrain, and her own limitations, Arunima pressed on, driven by a powerful inner resolve. Her climb was not just a test of endurance but a testament to human resilience and the power of dreams.

On May 21, 2013, Arunima Sinha became the first female amputee to scale Mount Everest, turning her personal tragedy into a triumphant story of courage and perseverance. Her achievement resonated far beyond the climbing community, inspiring millions around the world.

Arunima's story is a beacon of hope and inspiration, demonstrating that with determination and hard work, even the most daunting obstacles can be overcome. Her journey from the depths of despair to the pinnacle of the world stands as a powerful example of how one can rise above life's adversities to achieve greatness.

Fostering Creativity and Innovation

"Creativity is intelligence having fun."

- Albert Einstein

Encourage young people to think creatively and embrace innovation. Provide them with opportunities to explore their interests and develop their talents. Celebrate their creative efforts and encourage them to take risks and experiment with new ideas.

Exploring diverse interests can lead to groundbreaking innovations and profound impacts on various fields. There are stories of several renowned innovators whose multidisciplinary pursuits have significantly shaped their achievements. From technology to science, these individuals demonstrate how a broad spectrum of interests can drive creativity and success.

Steve Jobs: The Calligraphy Class That Changed Everything

Background and Influence: In 1972, Steve Jobs enrolled at Reed College and took a calligraphy class that profoundly influenced his design philosophy. This course introduced him to the beauty of typography and the importance of design aesthetics.

Impact on Apple:

- o **Macintosh:** Jobs integrated beautiful typography into the Macintosh, revolutionizing personal computing by making it accessible and visually appealing.

- o **Design Philosophy:** The emphasis on elegant design and user experience became a hallmark of Apple products, from the iPhone to the MacBook.

Elon Musk: The Polymath Entrepreneur

Background and Diverse Interests:

Elon Musk's education in physics and economics, combined with his curiosity about renewable energy, space exploration, and artificial intelligence, has driven his multifaceted career.

Impact:

- **Tesla:** Musk's interest in sustainable energy led to the creation of Tesla, revolutionizing the automotive industry with electric cars.
- **SpaceX:** His passion for space exploration resulted in SpaceX, aiming to make space travel more affordable and eventually enable human colonization of Mars.
- **Neuralink and The Boring Company:** These ventures showcase Musk's ambition to solve global issues through technological innovation.

Sergey Brin: The Multidisciplinary Innovator

Background and Diverse Interests:

Sergey Brin, co-founder of Google, has a background in mathematics, computer science, and elements of creative arts, leading to a unique approach to technology and innovation.

Impact:

- **Google:** Brin's expertise in algorithms revolutionized information access through Google Search.
- **Google X:** His interest in futuristic technologies led to projects like self-driving cars and Google Glass.

Mark Zuckerberg: The Hacker Philanthropist

Background and Diverse Interests:

Mark Zuckerberg's diverse interests in computer programming, psychology, and classical languages influenced his creation of Facebook and philanthropic endeavors.

Impact:

- **Facebook:** Zuckerberg combined programming skills with an understanding of human behavior, transforming global communication.
- **Philanthropy:** The Chan Zuckerberg Initiative tackles education and global health challenges, reflecting his broader interests.

Larry Page: The Innovator in Technology and Sustainability

Background and Diverse Interests:

Larry Page's background in computer engineering and environmental sustainability shaped his vision for Google and Alphabet Inc.

Impact:

- **Google Search:** Page's development of the PageRank algorithm transformed web search.
- **Alphabet Inc. :** Projects in renewable energy and life sciences showcase his commitment to sustainability and innovation.

Marie Curie: The Trailblazing Scientist

Background and Diverse Interests:

Marie Curie's interdisciplinary approach in physics and chemistry led to groundbreaking discoveries in radioactivity.

Impact:

- **Radioactivity Research:** Discoveries of radium and polonium advanced scientific understanding.
- **Medical Applications:** Curie's work laid the foundation for radiation use in cancer treatment.

Jeff Bezos: The Relentless Innovator

Background and Diverse Interests: Jeff Bezos, with a background in computer science and electrical engineering, pursued interests in space exploration and media.

Impact:

- **Amazon:** Revolutionized retail through e-commerce.
- **Blue Origin:** Aimed to make space travel accessible.
- **The Washington Post:** Revitalized journalism through digital innovation.

The stories of these innovators underscore the importance of encouraging young people to explore diverse interests. By fostering curiosity and supporting a wide range of learning experiences, we can cultivate the next generation of leaders and innovators capable of making significant contributions to society. The intersection of different fields often leads to unique insights, driving progress in ways that a singular focus might not achieve. Their stories highlight the importance of encouraging young people to explore diverse interests, as these experiences can lead to groundbreaking innovations.

Promoting Empathy and Compassion

"Empathy is about finding echoes of another person in yourself."

- Mohsin Hamid

Teach young people the value of empathy and compassion. Encourage them to understand and care about the experiences and feelings of others. Promote involvement in community service and acts of kindness, fostering a sense of social responsibility and connection.

The Story of Craig Kielburger: A Young Advocate for Children's Rights

Craig Kielburger's journey from a concerned 12-year-old to a globally recognized advocate for children's rights is a powerful testament to the impact one individual can have on the world. Inspired by a news article about child labor, Craig's empathy and determination led him to found Free the Children, an organization that has empowered millions of young people to engage in social activism and community service. This is the inspiring story of how one child's compassion sparked a global movement.

The Awakening: Discovering Child Labor

In 1995, Craig Kielburger was a typical 12-year-old living in Thornhill, Ontario, Canada. One morning, as he skimmed through the newspaper before school, a headline caught his eye: "Battled Child Labor, Boy, 12, Murdered." The article told the tragic story of Iqbal Masih, a young Pakistani boy who had been forced into labor at a carpet factory and later became an outspoken activist against child labor, only to be murdered at the age of 12.

This story struck a deep chord with Craig. He couldn't understand how a child his age could endure such suffering, and he was moved by Iqbal's courage in fighting against such injustice. The contrast between his own life and Iqbal's was stark and unsettling. Determined to learn more, Craig began researching child labor and human rights abuses around the world.

Taking Action: Founding Free the Children

Craig's research revealed the pervasive and horrific conditions faced by millions of children globally. He felt compelled to take action but quickly realized that he couldn't do it alone. He gathered a group of his classmates, and together they founded Free the Children, an organization dedicated to ending child labor and advocating for children's rights.

The group started small, holding bake sales and car washes to raise funds and awareness. They wrote letters to politicians, organized speaking engagements, and used every available platform to spread their message. Craig's passion and leadership were evident, and his story began to attract media attention, amplifying the reach of their cause.

Growing the Movement: From Local to Global

Free the Children's mission resonated with people around the world, and the organization grew rapidly. Craig's ability to connect with young people and inspire them to take action was a driving force behind this growth. He believed in the power of youth to effect change and worked tirelessly to empower young activists.

Key Milestones

1. International Advocacy: Craig traveled extensively, meeting with world leaders, including the Dalai Lama and Mother

Teresa, to advocate for children's rights. His dedication brought global attention to the issue of child labor.

2. Educational Programs: Free the Children launched educational programs and campaigns to raise awareness about child labor and promote children's rights. These programs empowered students to become informed advocates for change.

3. Me to We: In 2008, Craig and his brother Marc Kielburger co-founded Me to We, a social enterprise that provides socially conscious products and experiences, with profits supporting Free the Children. This initiative helped create sustainable funding for their projects and further engaged young people in social activism.

Impact: Empowering Millions

Under Craig's leadership, Free the Children evolved into WE Charity, a comprehensive organization focused on empowering youth through education, community development, and social entrepreneurship. WE Charity's initiatives have had a profound impact on millions of lives around the world.

Empowering Young People

WE Schools, a program developed by WE Charity, engages millions of students globally, encouraging them to participate in local and international service projects. These initiatives not only address critical social issues but also equip young people with leadership skills and a sense of global responsibility.

Transforming Communities

WE Villages, another key initiative, focuses on sustainable development in communities across Asia, Africa, and Latin

America. By addressing education, clean water, health, food security, and income opportunities, WE Villages empowers communities to break the cycle of poverty.

Global Reach

WE Charity's impact is far-reaching, with programs and initiatives in over 45 countries. The organization's commitment to sustainable change and youth empowerment has inspired a generation of young people to take action and make a difference in their communities and beyond.

Lessons from Craig Kielburger's Journey

Craig Kielburger's story offers several important lessons:

1. The Power of Empathy: Craig's journey began with a deep sense of empathy for other children's suffering. His ability to connect with the struggles of others fueled his passion for change.

2. Youth as Catalysts for Change: Craig's work demonstrates that young people have the potential to be powerful agents of change. By believing in their ability to make a difference, he empowered millions of youths to take action.

3. The Importance of Awareness: Raising awareness about social issues is a critical step toward change. Craig used his platform to educate others and inspire them to join the fight against child labor.

4. Sustainable Impact: Craig's commitment to sustainable development and community empowerment ensures that the changes initiated by WE Charity have a lasting impact.

Craig Kielburger's remarkable journey from a concerned 12-year-old to a global advocate for children's rights is a testament to the power of empathy, determination, and the potential of youth to effect change. His story reminds us that one person, regardless of age, can make a significant difference in the world. By encouraging young people to explore their passions and take action, we can inspire the next generation of leaders and changemakers. Craig's legacy lives on through the millions of young people he has empowered and the communities he has transformed, proving that age is no barrier to making a profound impact on the world.

Providing Mentorship and Guidance

"A mentor is someone who allows you to see the hope inside yourself."

- Oprah Winfrey

Mentorship is a powerful way to inspire young people. Offer your time, knowledge, and experience to guide them. Listen to their concerns, provide constructive feedback, and help them navigate their personal and professional journeys.

Maya Angelou was mentored by her mother, Vivian Baxter, who provided her with love, guidance, and support. This mentorship helped Angelou overcome her early traumas and become a celebrated poet and author. Angelou's story illustrates the profound impact a mentor can have on a young person's life.

Encouraging Lifelong Learning

"Live as if you were to die tomorrow. Learn as if you were to live forever."

- Mahatma Gandhi

Instill a love of learning in young people. Encourage curiosity and the pursuit of knowledge in all its forms. Highlight the importance of education and continuous self-improvement as tools for personal and professional growth.

The Story of Dr. E. Sreedharan: Engineering Marvels with Curiosity and Passion

Dr. Elattuvalapil Sreedharan, popularly known as the "Metro Man of India," is a shining example of how curiosity, passion, and dedication can lead to transformative achievements. His work in developing India's urban transportation systems, particularly the Delhi Metro, has revolutionized public transport in the country. This chapter explores the life and contributions of Dr. Sreedharan, highlighting how his relentless pursuit of engineering excellence has created lasting impacts.

Early Life: The Foundation of Curiosity

Dr. Sreedharan was born on June 12, 1932, in the village of Karukaputhur in Kerala, India. From a young age, he displayed a keen interest in science and engineering. His curiosity about how things worked led him to pursue a degree in civil engineering from the Government Engineering College in Kakinada, Andhra Pradesh.

A Humble Beginning

After completing his education, Sreedharan joined the Indian Railways as a probationary assistant engineer in 1954. His early assignments, including the restoration of the Pamban Bridge in Tamil Nadu, showcased his engineering prowess and problem-solving abilities. This project earned him recognition and set the stage for his future achievements.

Engineering Marvels: Curiosity Meets Innovation

Dr. Sreedharan's career is marked by a series of engineering marvels that have had a profound impact on India's infrastructure and public transportation.

The Konkan Railway: A Feat of Engineering

One of Sreedharan's most significant achievements was the construction of the Konkan Railway, a 760-kilometer stretch of rail line along India's western coast. This project, completed in the 1990s, was a massive engineering challenge due to the difficult terrain, numerous rivers, and environmental concerns.

Innovative Solutions:

- **Tunnel Construction:** The project involved constructing 92 tunnels and 179 major bridges, requiring innovative engineering techniques.

- **Project Management:** Sreedharan's leadership ensured that the project was completed in a record seven years, despite the challenges.

The Delhi Metro: Transforming Urban Transport

Dr. Sreedharan's most iconic contribution is the development of the Delhi Metro. Appointed as the managing director of the Delhi Metro Rail Corporation (DMRC) in 1997, he was tasked with implementing a modern metro system in the capital city.

Impact on Public Transport:

- **Efficiency and Punctuality:** Under Sreedharan's leadership, the Delhi Metro became known for its efficiency, cleanliness, and punctuality, setting new standards for public transport in India.

- **Technological Advancements:** He introduced state-of-the-art technology and practices, ensuring the metro system was world-class.

- **Environmental Benefits:** The metro has significantly reduced traffic congestion and air pollution in Delhi, improving the quality of life for millions of residents.

Expanding the Metro Network

Inspired by the success of the Delhi Metro, other cities in India sought Sreedharan's expertise to develop their metro systems. His work extended to projects in Kochi, Jaipur, and Lucknow, further revolutionizing urban transportation across the country.

The Role of Passion and Perseverance

Dr. Sreedharan's journey was not without obstacles. His passion for engineering and unwavering perseverance enabled him to overcome numerous challenges and achieve remarkable success.

Tackling Challenges

Whether it was the tough terrains of the Konkan coast or the urban complexities of Delhi, Sreedharan faced numerous technical, logistical, and bureaucratic challenges. His problem-solving skills and innovative mindset were crucial in addressing these issues effectively.

Commitment to Excellence

Sreedharan's commitment to excellence was evident in every project he undertook. He emphasized meticulous planning, adherence to timelines, and maintaining high-quality standards, ensuring that every project was completed efficiently and effectively.

Legacy: A Lasting Impact

Dr. Sreedharan's contributions have left a lasting impact on India's infrastructure and public transportation systems. His work has transformed urban mobility, making cities more connected and accessible.

Transforming Lives

The metro systems developed under Sreedharan's leadership have transformed the daily commute for millions of Indians. They provide a reliable, safe, and efficient mode of transport, improving the quality of life in urban areas.

Inspiring Future Engineers

Dr. Sreedharan's story is an inspiration for aspiring engineers and professionals. His dedication, curiosity, and passion for engineering serve as a guiding light for those who seek to make a positive impact through their work.

Recognitions and Awards

In recognition of his contributions, Dr. Sreedharan has received numerous awards and honors, including the Padma Shri in 2001 and the Padma Vibhushan in 2008, two of India's highest civilian awards. His achievements have earned him respect and admiration both nationally and internationally.

Dr. E. Sreedharan's life and achievements are a testament to the power of curiosity and passion in driving innovation and excellence. From the challenging terrains of the Konkan Railway to the bustling streets of Delhi, his engineering marvels have transformed India's infrastructure and urban transportation. His story reminds us that with curiosity, passion, and perseverance, we can overcome challenges and create lasting, positive change. Dr.

Sreedharan's legacy continues to inspire and guide future generations of engineers and innovators, proving that one individual's vision and dedication can leave an indelible mark on the world.

Conclusion: Inspiring a Brighter Future

Inspiring young people is about more than imparting knowledge; it's about lighting a fire within them that will burn brightly throughout their lives. By being role models, encouraging dreams, teaching resilience, fostering creativity, promoting empathy, providing mentorship, and encouraging lifelong learning, we can guide young people to achieve their fullest potential.

When you meet young people, remember that your influence can shape their futures in profound ways. Inspire them to be their best selves, and in doing so, contribute to a brighter, more hopeful world. The ripple effect of your influence can lead to significant positive changes in individuals and communities, ultimately creating a better future for all.

Chapter- 2

Educate the Future by Educating Children

Education is one of the most powerful tools we can offer the next generation. When you meet children, every interaction is an opportunity to educate them—not just academically, but also morally, socially, and emotionally. This chapter explores the multifaceted nature of education and provides practical strategies, examples, and inspiration to help you educate children effectively.

Nurturing Seeds of Knowledge and Kindness

In the heart of a bustling capital of Jharkhand, Ranchi city, Father Norbert encountered a group of children whose lives would forever leave an imprint on his understanding of education's transformative power. As a volunteer at a local community center, he had the privilege of leading educational workshops for underprivileged children once in six months.

Among these children was Rahul, a bright-eyed boy with a curiosity that knew no bounds. His enthusiasm for learning was infectious, and he soaked up knowledge like a sponge. However, beyond academic lessons, Rahul and his peers taught Father Norbert invaluable lessons about the holistic nature of education.

During one session focused on storytelling, Father Norbert shared a tale of perseverance and kindness. The story resonated deeply with the children, sparking discussions about empathy and compassion. Rahul, in particular, surprised me with his insightful questions and empathetic responses. It became clear that education was not just about textbooks and exams; it was about nurturing empathy, resilience, and moral integrity.

As weeks turned into months, Father Norbert witnessed firsthand the transformative impact of holistic education on Rahul and his friends. Through interactive activities, we explored themes of teamwork, respect for diversity, and environmental stewardship. Each session was a reminder that education extends beyond the classroom walls, it encompasses the development of critical thinking, emotional intelligence, and ethical values.

One memorable afternoon, Rahul approached Father Norbert with a handmade card adorned with vibrant colors and heartfelt words of gratitude. He expressed how the sessions had ignited a passion for learning within him and inspired him to dream big. His words touched the heart of Father Norbert and reaffirmed his belief in the profound influence educators can have on young minds.

Despite the challenges they faced outside the community center poverty, violence, and social inequality Rahul and his friends demonstrated resilience and a hunger for knowledge. They taught Father Norbert that education is not just a privilege but a fundamental right that empowers children to break the cycle of poverty and build brighter futures.

Years later, Father Norbert still cherishes the memories of those transformative moments with Rahul and his peers. They taught

Father Norbert that education is a journey of mutual growth, where educators impart knowledge and values, and children inspire with their curiosity, resilience, and boundless potential.

Practical Strategies for Educating Children Effectively

Create Engaging Learning Environments: Use interactive and creative teaching methods to keep children engaged and enthusiastic about learning.

Integrate Moral and Social Education: Incorporate discussions and activities that promote empathy, respect, teamwork, and environmental stewardship.

Encourage Critical Thinking: Foster a culture of questioning and exploration to develop children's analytical and problem-solving skills.

Promote Emotional Intelligence: Teach children to identify and manage their emotions, empathize with others, and build positive relationships.

Celebrate Diversity: Embrace and celebrate cultural, ethnic, and religious diversity to cultivate a sense of inclusion and mutual respect among children.

Educating children goes beyond imparting knowledge; it is about shaping compassionate, resilient, and socially responsible individuals who will contribute positively to society. Rahul and his friends taught me that each child is a beacon of potential, waiting to be nurtured and empowered through meaningful education. Their journey continues to inspire me to advocate for inclusive, holistic education that nurtures the mind, heart, and spirit of every child.

The Importance of Education

"Education is the most powerful weapon which you can use to change the world."

- Nelson Mandela

Education goes beyond the confines of traditional schooling. It is about equipping children with the skills, knowledge, and values they need to navigate life and contribute positively to society. When you meet children, whether in a classroom, at home, or in the community, your role as an educator is crucial in shaping their future.

Encouraging Curiosity and Lifelong Learning

"Tell me and I forget, teach me and I may remember, involve me and I learn."

- Benjamin Franklin

Children are naturally curious. Encouraging this curiosity fosters a love for learning that lasts a lifetime. Create environments where questions are welcomed, and exploration is encouraged. Provide them with resources, opportunities, and experiences that stimulate their minds and ignite their passion for discovery.

Thomas Edison's mother, Nancy Edison, played a critical role in his early education. When Edison's teachers labeled him as a difficult child, his mother decided to homeschool him. She nurtured his curiosity, allowing him to conduct experiments at home. This supportive environment helped Edison become one of the greatest inventors in history.

Teaching Core Academic Skills

"Education is not the filling of a pail, but the lighting of a fire."

- William Butler Yeats

While fostering curiosity is essential, teaching core academic skills forms the foundation of a child's education. Focus on literacy, numeracy, and critical thinking. Use engaging and interactive methods to make learning enjoyable and effective. Tailor your approach to meet each child's unique learning style and pace.

Maria Montessori developed the Montessori method of education, which emphasizes hands-on learning and self-directed activity. Her approach allows children to develop academic skills through exploration and discovery, fostering both independence and a deep understanding of the subjects they study.

Imparting Values and Morals

"Educating the mind without educating the heart is no education at all."

- Aristotle

Education should encompass moral and ethical instruction. Teach children values such as honesty, kindness, respect, and responsibility. Use stories, role-playing, and real-life examples to illustrate these values in action. Encourage discussions about right and wrong to help children develop a strong moral compass.

Fred Rogers, host of "Mister Rogers' Neighborhood," used his television program to teach children important life lessons about kindness, empathy, and understanding. His gentle, thoughtful approach helped children learn how to navigate their emotions and interactions with others in a positive way.

Developing Social Skills and Emotional Intelligence

"Emotional intelligence is the ability to make emotions work for you, instead of against you."

- Travis Bradberry

Social skills and emotional intelligence are crucial for a child's personal and professional success. Teach children how to communicate effectively, resolve conflicts, and understand their own emotions and those of others. Activities like group projects, role-playing, and reflective discussions can enhance these skills.

The "Second Step" program is an educational curriculum designed to improve social-emotional skills in children. It teaches empathy, emotion management, and problem-solving, helping children build strong relationships and navigate social challenges effectively.

Promoting Physical Health and Wellness

"To keep the body in good health is a duty... otherwise we shall not be able to keep our mind strong and clear."

- Buddha

Education should also address physical health and wellness. Teach children the importance of regular exercise, a balanced diet, and good hygiene. Incorporate physical activities into their daily routine and educate them about making healthy lifestyle choices.

Michelle Obama's "Let's Move!" campaign aimed to combat childhood obesity by encouraging healthier food choices and more physical activity. The initiative provided resources and support to schools, parents, and communities to promote a healthier lifestyle for children.

Encouraging Creativity and Innovation

"Creativity is the key to success in the future, and primary education is where teachers can bring creativity in children at that level."

- A. P. J. Abdul Kalam

Nurturing creativity helps children develop problem-solving skills and innovative thinking. Provide opportunities for artistic expression, creative writing, and imaginative play. Encourage children to think outside the box and explore new ideas without fear of failure.

The Reggio Emilia approach to early childhood education emphasizes creativity and critical thinking. Children are encouraged to express themselves through various forms of art and play, fostering an environment where creative thinking thrives.

Providing Mentorship and Guidance

"A mentor is someone who sees more talent and ability within you than you see in yourself, and helps bring it out of you."

- Bob Proctor

Mentorship is a powerful aspect of education. Be a guide and mentor to children, offering wisdom, support, and encouragement. Share your experiences and insights to help them navigate their own paths. A mentor's belief in a child's potential can be transformative.

Jaime Escalante, a high school math teacher, became famous for his work with students at Garfield High School in East Los Angeles. Despite many students being labeled as "unteachable," Escalante's belief in their potential and his innovative teaching methods led them to excel in Advanced Placement calculus, inspiring future generations.

Embracing Diversity and Inclusion

"Diversity is the one true thing we all have in common. Celebrate it every day."

- Author Unknown

Teach children to appreciate and respect diversity in all its forms. Foster an inclusive environment where every child feels valued and accepted. Encourage open-mindedness and understanding by exposing children to different cultures, perspectives, and experiences.

The International Baccalaureate (IB) program emphasizes global-mindedness and cultural understanding. It encourages students to engage with diverse perspectives and develop a respect for people from all backgrounds, preparing them to be compassionate global citizens.

Conclusion: Educating for a Brighter Future

When you meet children, remember that each interaction is an opportunity to educate and inspire. By encouraging curiosity, teaching core skills, imparting values, developing social and emotional intelligence, promoting health, nurturing creativity, providing mentorship, and embracing diversity, you equip children with the tools they need to thrive.

Your efforts in educating children not only shape their futures but also contribute to a more enlightened, compassionate, and innovative world. Embrace the role of educator with enthusiasm and commitment, knowing that you are making a lasting impact on the lives of the next generation.

Chapter-3

Always Help the Elderly

In a world that often prioritizes the young and the new, it is crucial to remember the value and wisdom that older generations bring. Helping the elderly is not just a moral obligation but an opportunity to learn, connect, and give back. This chapter explores the various ways we can assist older people to guide you in making a positive impact.

A Heartfelt Bond with Mr. and Mrs. Thompson Peter

Mr. and Mrs. Thompson Peter were a couple who had spent their lives together, weathering the storms of time and nurturing a bond that transcended decades. In their twilight years, they found themselves in an old age home, their children settled far away in England. Despite the physical distance, their faith and commitment to their Sunday routine at Queen of Peace Cathedral remained unwavering.

Father Norbert first encountered Mr. and Mrs. Thompson Peter during one Sunday Mass. They arrived hand in hand, their faces reflecting a lifetime of shared moments and enduring love. Over time, their paths crossed more frequently, and he became drawn to the warmth and wisdom the elderly couple.

One chilly Sunday afternoon after Mass, Father Norbert noticed Mr. and Mrs. Thompson Peter struggling to navigate the steps outside the church. Without hesitation, he approached Mr. & Mrs. Thompson and offered a ride back to the old age home in his own vehicle. They gratefully accepted, and during the short journey, they shared stories Father Norbert of their youth, their family, and the cherished memories that sustained the couple.

That simple act of kindness forged a connection that surpassed generations. From that day forward, Mr. and Mrs. Thompson adopted Fahter Norbert as their surrogate son. They showered him with wisdom and affection, offering guidance and support in ways that touched his heart. They became his mentors, teaching him about resilience, faith, and the importance of cherishing every moment.

As weeks turned into months, Father Norbert continued to assist Mr. and Mrs. Thompson, helping with errands, accompanying them on walks through the old age home's gardens, and sharing laughter over cups of tea. Their Sundays together became a cherished ritual, filled with stories, lessons, and the warmth of genuine companionship.

Then, tragedy struck. The COVID-19 pandemic swept through the parish community, and despite the community efforts to protect them, Mr. and Mrs. Thompson fell ill. The virus claimed their lives, leaving behind a void in their hearts and our church.

Reflecting on their time together, Father Norbert realized the profound impact that their relationship had on him. Through helping Mr. and Mrs. Thompson, he had gained far more than he had given. Their love, wisdom, and unwavering faith had shaped Father Norbert's values and enriched his life in ways he could never have anticipated.

The lessons Father Norbert learned from Mr. and Mrs. Thompson Peter continue to guide him:

- **Compassionate Care:**

Providing assistance to older people is not just about physical help but also about offering compassion, companionship, and emotional support.

- **Respect and Dignity:**

Older adults deserve to be treated with respect and dignity, honoring their contributions and valuing their perspectives.

- **Legacy of Wisdom:**

By listening to and learning from older individuals like Mr. and Mrs. Thompson, we inherit valuable wisdom that shapes our values, decisions, and actions.

- **Gratitude:**

Expressing gratitude for the wisdom and guidance of older generations honors their contributions and ensures their legacy lives on.

Strategies for Making a Positive Impact

The Importance of Helping the Elderly

"The true measure of any society can be found in how it treats its most vulnerable members."

- Mahatma Gandhi

Older adults have contributed significantly to society throughout their lives. Helping them in their later years is a way of honoring their contributions and ensuring they live with dignity and respect. Providing assistance can range from offering practical help to providing emotional support and companionship.

Offering Practical Assistance

"Too often we underestimate the power of a touch, a smile, a kind word, a listening ear, an honest compliment, or the smallest act of caring, all of which have the potential to turn a life around."

- Leo Buscaglia

Many elderly individuals face challenges with mobility, health, and daily tasks. Offering practical help can make a significant difference in their quality of life. This can include running errands, helping with household chores, or assisting with medical appointments.

Meals on Wheels is a program that delivers nutritious meals to homebound seniors. Volunteers not only provide food but also offer a friendly visit and a safety check, addressing both the nutritional and social needs of the elderly.

Providing Emotional Support

"Sometimes, reaching out and taking someone's hand is the beginning of a journey. At other times, it is allowing another to take yours."

- Vera Nazarian

Loneliness and isolation are common issues among the elderly. Providing emotional support through regular visits, phone calls, or even simple gestures of kindness can have a profound impact.

Listening to their stories and showing genuine interest in their lives fosters connection and reduces feelings of isolation.

The "Adopt a Grandparent" initiative pairs volunteers with elderly individuals who lack family connections. Through regular visits and activities, these relationships provide much-needed companionship and emotional support.

Respecting and Valuing Their Wisdom

"Respect for ourselves guides our morals; respect for others guides our manners."

- Laurence Sterne

Older adults possess a wealth of knowledge and experience. Valuing their wisdom and learning from their experiences not only honors them but enriches our own lives. Encourage intergenerational conversations where they can share their stories, insights, and advice.

StoryCorps is a nonprofit organization that records and preserves personal stories. Many of these stories come from older adults, capturing their experiences and preserving their wisdom for future generations. This initiative highlights the value of listening to and learning from the elderly.

Promoting Independence

"Helping one person might not change the whole world, but it could change the world for one person."

- Unknown

While providing assistance is important, promoting independence is equally vital. Empower older adults by encouraging them to engage in activities that they can manage on their own. Offer support that enables them to maintain their independence and dignity.

Senior centers offer a variety of programs and activities that promote physical and mental well-being. These centers provide a space where older adults can participate in exercise classes, hobby groups, and social events, fostering both independence and community.

Ensuring Their Safety and Comfort

"To care for those who once cared for us is one of the highest honors."

- Tia Walker

Ensuring the safety and comfort of elderly individuals is crucial. This can involve making home modifications to prevent falls, assisting with medication management, and ensuring they have access to necessary healthcare services. Safety and comfort are fundamental to their well-being.

The "Lifeline" program offers medical alert systems that allow elderly individuals to call for help with the push of a button. This technology provides peace of mind for both the elderly and their families, knowing that help is readily available in an emergency.

Fostering Social Connections

"Aging is not lost youth but a new stage of opportunity and strength."

- Betty Friedan

Encouraging social connections helps combat loneliness and depression among the elderly. Facilitate opportunities for them to engage with their peers, participate in community events, and stay connected with family and friends. Social interaction is vital for mental and emotional health.

The "Elder Orphan" Facebook group connects older adults who live alone and have limited family support. This online community provides a platform for social interaction, mutual support, and the sharing of resources and advice.

Providing Resources and Advocacy

"Justice in the life and conduct of the State is possible only as first it resides in the hearts and souls of the citizens."

- Plato

Advocate for the needs and rights of the elderly. Provide them with information about available resources, such as healthcare, financial assistance, and legal support. Stand up against ageism and work towards creating a society that values and supports its older members.

The AARP (American Association of Retired Persons) offers various resources and advocacy for older adults. They provide information on health, retirement, and financial planning, and advocate for policies that benefit the elderly.

Conclusion: Creating a Compassionate Community

Helping the elderly is a responsibility that enriches both the giver and the receiver. By offering practical assistance, providing emotional support, valuing their wisdom, promoting independence, ensuring safety and comfort, fostering social connections, and advocating for their needs, we create a compassionate and inclusive community.

Every interaction with an older adult is an opportunity to make a positive difference. Embrace these opportunities with empathy, respect, and a genuine desire to help. By doing so, we honor the past, enrich the present, and pave the way for a more caring and connected future.

Chapter-4

Inheriting the Wisdom of the Ages

In our journey through life, we encounter individuals whose wisdom stands out a testament to their experiences, insights, and reflections. These wise individuals are living repositories of knowledge, offering lessons that can profoundly shape our understanding and actions. This chapter explores the importance of studying wise people to guide you in harnessing their wisdom.

Father Joseph was a senior priest at the parish where Father Tom a young priest began his ministry fresh out of seminary. Father Joseph's presence commanded respect to Fr. Tom not just because of his age and tenure but because of the profound wisdom he carried within him. Tall and dignified, Father Joseph had a gentle demeanor that immediately put people at ease. His deep, resonant voice carried the weight of years spent in service to the church and community.

The young priest Father Tom first encountered Father Joseph during his early days before his priestly ordination. Nervous and eager to prove himself, he often sought his advice on matters ranging from pastoral care to handling parish activities. Father Joseph always listened patiently, his wise eyes twinkling with understanding. He had a knack for simplifying complex issues and offering practical solutions grounded in both faith and experience.

One winter evening, as Father Tom and Father Joseph sat sipping tea, the junior priest confided in Father Joseph about his struggles with balancing pastoral duties and personal life. He admitted feeling overwhelmed by the demands of ministry and doubted whether he was making a meaningful impact. Instead of offering quick fixes, Father Joseph shared stories from his own journey- tales to his junior companion of doubt and perseverance, moments of joy and profound spiritual growth.

"Remember, my son," Father Joseph said gently to Father Tom, "ministry is not about perfection but about presence. Being present to your flock in their joys and sorrows, in their doubts and triumphs that's where the true essence of service lies."

Father Joseph's wisdom extended beyond pastoral advice. He taught his younger companion the importance of humility in leadership, the power of listening without judgment, and the significance of prayer as a foundation for all actions. His insights were not just theoretical teachings but lived experiences that shaped his approach to ministry and life.

Throughout the years under Father Joseph's mentorship, Fr. Tom witnessed how his wisdom touched lives. Parishioners sought him out for guidance, not just on spiritual matters but on matters of the heart and soul. His sermons were filled with timeless wisdom and practical advice that resonated with people of all ages and backgrounds.

Father Joseph's legacy of wisdom continues to inspire Father Tom today as he navigates the challenges and joys of priesthood. His lessons on faith, compassion, and perseverance serve as guiding principles in Fathrer Tom's own ministry, reminding him that true wisdom is not just learned but lived.

Through Father Joseph, Tom learned several key lessons about inheriting wisdom:

1. The Power of Presence:

Father Joseph taught that true ministry begins with being present—fully and authentically present—to those entrusted for care.

2. Humility in Leadership:

He exemplified humility in leadership, showing Father Tom that true authority comes from service and compassion rather than from a position of power.

3. Patience and Understanding:

Father Joseph's patience and understanding taught Tom the importance of listening attentively and responding with empathy to the needs of others.

4. Perseverance and Faith:

His stories of perseverance through adversity strengthened the junior priest faith and taught him to trust in God's guidance even in uncertain times.

5. Legacy of Wisdom:

By embracing and internalizing Father Joseph's wisdom, Tom strives to honor his legacy and pass on these invaluable lessons to future generations of priests and parishioners.

Strategies for Harnessing Wisdom

Inheriting the wisdom of the ages through mentors like Father Joseph enriches our lives and strengthens our ability to serve others with compassion, humility, and faith. By studying and internalizing their wisdom, we honor their contributions and ensure that their teachings continue to inspire and guide us on our journey of faith and service.

The Value of Wisdom

"Wisdom is not a product of schooling but of the lifelong attempt to acquire it."

- Albert Einstein

Wisdom encompasses a deep understanding of life, gained through diverse experiences and thoughtful reflection. It is more than knowledge; it involves discernment, insight, and the ability to make sound judgments. Studying wise people allows us to tap into their well of knowledge, enriching our own lives and perspectives.

Listening Actively and Reflectively

"Most people do not listen with the intent to understand; they listen with the intent to reply."

- Stephen R. Covey

When interacting with wise individuals, practice active and reflective listening. This means fully engaging with their words, asking thoughtful questions, and considering the implications of their insights. Avoid the urge to interrupt or offer your opinions prematurely; instead, absorb their wisdom with an open mind.

Socrates, one of history's wisest philosophers, utilized the Socratic method, which involved asking probing questions to stimulate critical thinking and illuminate ideas. By adopting a similar approach, we can delve deeper into the wisdom of others, uncovering valuable insights.

Observing Actions and Behaviors

"Actions speak louder than words."

- Proverb

Wisdom is often demonstrated through actions as much as words. Observe how wise individuals handle challenges, make decisions, and interact with others. Their behaviors can provide practical lessons on leadership, empathy, resilience, and integrity.

Mahatma Gandhi's life exemplified wisdom in action. His principles of non-violence and civil disobedience, combined with his personal integrity and humility, offer profound lessons. Studying his life, one learns the power of peaceful resistance and the importance of aligning actions with values.

Engaging in Deep Conversations

"Wise men speak because they have something to say; fools because they have to say something."

- Plato

Engage wise individuals in meaningful conversations that go beyond superficial topics. Discuss life's profound questions, seek their perspectives on complex issues, and explore their life experiences. These conversations can be enlightening and transformative.

The friendship between author J.R.R. Tolkien and C.S. Lewis led to deep, philosophical discussions about literature, religion, and life. Their dialogues not only enriched their own writings but also provided a fertile ground for exploring significant ideas and beliefs.

Learning from Their Mistakes and Successes

"Experience is simply the name we give our mistakes."

- Oscar Wilde

Wise people often have a wealth of experiences, including both successes and failures. Learn from their journeys, understanding the lessons they gleaned from their mistakes and triumphs. This can provide valuable guidance and prevent you from making similar errors.

Thomas Edison, one of the most prolific inventors, experienced numerous failures before achieving success. His perspective on failure as a learning opportunity is encapsulated in his famous quote: "I have not failed. I've just found 10,000 ways that won't work." Studying Edison's resilience and innovative mindset offers lessons in perseverance and creativity.

Reading Their Works and Teachings

"Books are the quietest and most constant of friends; they are the most accessible and wisest of counselors, and the most patient of teachers."

- Charles W. Eliot

Many wise individuals have documented their thoughts, philosophies, and experiences in books, articles, and speeches. Reading their works allows you to access their wisdom at your own pace and reflect deeply on their teachings.

Marcus Aurelius, the Roman Emperor, and philosopher, left behind a treasure trove of wisdom in his work "Meditations." This collection of personal writings offers timeless reflections on leadership, ethics, and personal growth, providing a rich source of wisdom for readers.

Seeking Mentorship

"A mentor is someone who sees more talent and ability within you than you see in yourself, and helps bring it out of you."

- Bob Proctor

If possible, seek mentorship from wise individuals. A mentor can provide personalized guidance, share their experiences, and offer support tailored to your growth and development. Building a mentoring relationship allows for a deeper exchange of wisdom.

Steve Jobs was mentored by Mike Markkula, an early investor and executive at Apple. Markkula's guidance in business strategy and management was instrumental in shaping Jobs' approach to innovation and leadership. This mentorship highlights the transformative power of learning from someone with greater experience and insight.

Reflecting on Their Advice

"Knowing yourself is the beginning of all wisdom."

- Aristotle

Reflect on the advice and teachings you receive from wise individuals. Consider how their insights apply to your own life and circumstances. Personal reflection helps internalize their wisdom, making it more impactful and actionable.

Nelson Mandela's reflections on forgiveness and reconciliation after decades of imprisonment provide profound lessons in leadership and humanity. By contemplating his approach to conflict resolution and peacebuilding, individuals can apply these principles to their own lives and leadership styles.

Integrating Wisdom into Daily Life

"The only true wisdom is in knowing you know nothing."

- Socrates

True learning from wise people involves integrating their wisdom into your daily life. Apply their lessons in your decisions, actions, and interactions. Continually seek to grow and adapt, using their insights as a foundation for your own wisdom.

The Dalai Lama's teachings on compassion and mindfulness can be integrated into daily practices. By adopting a compassionate mindset and incorporating mindfulness into daily routines, individuals can enhance their well-being and relationships, embodying the wisdom of these teachings.

Conclusion: The Journey of Lifelong Learning

Meeting and studying wise people is an invaluable part of personal and intellectual growth. By actively listening, observing, engaging in deep conversations, learning from their experiences, reading their works, seeking mentorship, reflecting on their advice, and integrating their wisdom into daily life, we can enrich our own lives profoundly.

Wisdom is a journey, not a destination. Embrace the opportunity to learn from those who have walked the path before you. In doing so, you honor their experiences and equip yourself with the tools to navigate life's complexities with greater understanding and insight.

Chapter- 5

Applauding Leadership Prowess

Leaders play a pivotal role in shaping societies, organizations, and movements. Their vision, decisions, and actions influence many, and their responsibilities often come with significant challenges. Honoring leaders not only acknowledges their contributions but also fosters a culture of respect and gratitude. This chapter explores the importance of honoring leaders to guide you in recognizing and appreciating effective leadership.

In a bustling high school of a metropolis, there was a student named Maya Patel who stood out not only for her academic achievements but also for her exceptional leadership skills. Maya was known for her kindness, empathy, and the ability to bring people together, qualities that would shape her role as a student leader.

As the president of the student council, Maya took her responsibilities seriously. She initiated several impactful projects that benefited both students and the community. One such project was the establishment of a peer tutoring program aimed at supporting struggling students academically. Maya personally recruited volunteer tutors, organized tutoring sessions, and ensured that every student had access to the help they needed.

Beyond academics, Maya was passionate about fostering inclusivity and celebrating diversity within the school. She organized cultural exchange events, where students from different backgrounds shared their traditions and experiences. These events not only promoted understanding but also created a sense of unity among the diverse student body.

Maya's leadership was most evident during a challenging period when the school faced budget cuts that threatened extracurricular activities and student resources. Instead of succumbing to despair, Maya mobilized her fellow student council members and organized a series of fundraising initiatives. From bake sales to talent shows, Maya led with enthusiasm and determination, inspiring both students and staff to rally behind the cause.

Under Maya's guidance, the student council successfully raised enough funds to not only preserve essential programs but also introduce new initiatives that enriched the school community. Maya's ability to lead with empathy, resilience, and creativity earned her the admiration and respect of her peers and teachers alike.

What stood out most about Maya was her genuine care for others and her commitment to making a positive impact. She didn't seek recognition or praise but instead focused on creating meaningful change and supporting her fellow students.

Through Maya's leadership, we learn several invaluable lessons:

1. Empathy and Compassion:

Maya demonstrated that true leadership begins with empathy and compassion for others' needs and challenges. By understanding and addressing the concerns of her peers, she built trust and unity within the student body.

2. Initiative and Innovation:

Maya's proactive approach to problem-solving showed that leaders should not wait for solutions but actively seek opportunities to make a difference. Her creative fundraising ideas and community-building initiatives were instrumental in overcoming obstacles.

3. Inclusivity and Diversity:

Maya celebrated diversity and promoted inclusivity, recognizing the strength that comes from embracing different perspectives and experiences. Her efforts fostered a welcoming environment where every student felt valued and respected.

4. Resilience and Determination:

During difficult times, Maya's resilience and determination inspired others to persevere and remain focused on their goals. Her positive attitude and unwavering commitment were key factors in overcoming challenges and achieving success.

5. Leading by Example:

Maya led by example, embodying the values of integrity, humility, and dedication. Her actions spoke louder than words, earning her the trust and admiration of her peers and leaving a lasting impact on the school community.

Strategies for Honoring Student Leaders

Honoring student leaders like Maya Patel not only celebrates their individual achievements but also inspires others to lead with compassion, resilience, and a commitment to positive change. By recognizing and applauding their leadership prowess, we cultivate a culture where leadership is valued and nurtured, paving the way for a brighter future for all.

In honoring leaders, we recognize the immense responsibility they shoulder and the positive impact they have on our lives and organizations. By celebrating their strengths and supporting their vision, we foster a culture of respect, collaboration, and gratitude, paving the way for collective success and fulfillment.

The Significance of Applauding Leaders

"Leadership is not about being in charge. It is about taking care of those in your charge."

- Simon Sinek

Applauding leaders is about recognizing the weight of their responsibilities and the impact of their efforts. It involves showing appreciation for their guidance, support, and sacrifices. By honoring leaders, we affirm their positive influence and encourage continued excellence and integrity in leadership roles.

Acknowledging Their Contributions

"To handle yourself, use your head; to handle others, use your heart."

- Eleanor Roosevelt

Leaders often work tirelessly behind the scenes to ensure the success and well-being of their teams or communities. Acknowledging their contributions—whether through public recognition, awards, or simple expressions of thanks—validates their efforts and boosts their morale.

Let us consider the annual Nobel Prizes, which honor individuals who have made significant contributions to humanity in various fields. These prestigious awards highlight the importance of acknowledging outstanding achievements and inspire others to strive for excellence.

Showing Respect and Gratitude

"Respect is how to treat everyone, not just those you want to impress."

- Richard Branson

Respect and gratitude are fundamental in honoring leaders. This can be expressed through words and actions that demonstrate appreciation for their leadership. Simple gestures, such as a handwritten note or a public acknowledgment, can significantly impact leaders and reinforce their commitment to their roles.

In many cultures, it is customary to bow or salute leaders as a sign of respect. In Japan, for instance, bowing is a traditional way of showing respect and gratitude, reflecting the high regard for leadership and hierarchy in society.

Learning from Their Example

"A leader is one who knows the way, goes the way, and shows the way."

- John C. Maxwell

Honoring leaders involves recognizing their role as exemplars. Study their approaches, decisions, and behaviors to learn valuable lessons in leadership. By understanding what makes them effective, you can apply these insights to your own leadership journey.

Mahatma Gandhi's leadership in the Indian independence movement is studied worldwide for its principles of non-violence and civil disobedience. His example teaches the power of ethical leadership and the importance of aligning actions with core values.

Supporting Their Vision

"The best way to find yourself is to lose yourself in the service of others."

- Mahatma Gandhi

Leaders often have a vision that drives their actions and decisions. Supporting this vision shows respect for their leadership and contributes to the greater good. Engage actively with their initiatives, provide constructive feedback, and offer your skills and resources to help achieve common goals.

The followers of Martin Luther King Jr. supported his vision of civil rights through peaceful protests, advocacy, and community organization. Their collective efforts helped bring about significant social change, demonstrating the power of supporting a leader's vision.

Providing Constructive Feedback

"Feedback is the breakfast of champions."

- Ken Blanchard

Constructive feedback is essential for leaders to grow and improve. Honoring leaders includes offering honest, respectful feedback that helps them refine their strategies and approaches. This demonstrates your investment in their success and the success of the group or organization they lead.

In the business world, effective leaders like Warren Buffett seek and value feedback from their teams and stakeholders. This openness to constructive criticism helps them make informed decisions and foster a culture of continuous improvement.

Celebrating Their Successes

"Success is not final, failure is not fatal: It is the courage to continue that counts."

- Winston Churchill

Celebrating leaders' successes reinforces their achievements and motivates them to continue their efforts. Organize celebrations, write articles, or create social media posts highlighting their accomplishments. Public recognition not only honors leaders but also sets a positive example for others.

When NASA's Apollo 11 mission successfully landed on the moon, the astronauts, including Neil Armstrong, were celebrated as heroes. Parades, media coverage, and accolades honored their achievement, inspiring future generations of scientists and explorers.

Supporting Their Well-Being

"Leadership is not about being in charge. It is about taking care of those in your charge."

- Simon Sinek

Leadership can be stressful and demanding. Honoring leaders involves supporting their well-being, ensuring they have the resources and support needed to maintain their health and effectiveness. Encourage work-life balance, provide access to wellness programs, and offer emotional support.

Companies like Google and Apple offer wellness programs, including fitness centers, mental health resources, and flexible work schedules, to support the well-being of their leaders and employees. These initiatives recognize the importance of a healthy, balanced approach to leadership.

Building a Culture of Appreciation

> *"Appreciation can make a day, even change a life. Your willingness to put it into words is all that is necessary."*
>
> *- Margaret Cousins*

Creating a culture of appreciation within organizations and communities reinforces the importance of honoring leaders. Encourage regular expressions of gratitude, celebrate milestones, and recognize efforts at all levels. This fosters an environment where leaders and team members feel valued and motivated.

The Ritz-Carlton Hotel Company: A Culture of Appreciation and Recognition

The Ritz-Carlton Hotel Company is synonymous with luxury, impeccable service, and an unwavering commitment to excellence. One of the key elements that set the Ritz-Carlton apart from its competitors is its culture of appreciation and recognition. This culture not only ensures exceptional guest experiences but also fosters a motivated, loyal, and highly engaged workforce. In this article, we will explore the core principles of the Ritz-Carlton's culture, the strategies employed to cultivate appreciation and recognition, and the impact of these practices on both employees and guests.

The Gold Standards

At the heart of the Ritz-Carlton's culture are its "Gold Standards," a set of guiding principles that define the company's values and service philosophy. These standards include the Credo, the Motto, the Three Steps of Service, and the Employee Promise.

The Credo

The Credo is a declaration of the company's commitment to providing genuine care and comfort to its guests. It emphasizes the importance of fulfilling the needs and desires of guests while maintaining a warm and relaxed atmosphere.

The Motto

The Ritz-Carlton motto, "We are Ladies and Gentlemen serving Ladies and Gentlemen," encapsulates the essence of the company's service philosophy. It highlights the mutual respect and dignity with which employees and guests are treated, creating a culture of excellence and elegance.

The Three Steps of Service

The Three Steps of Service are simple yet powerful guidelines that ensure consistent and exceptional service:
1. A warm and sincere greeting using the guest's name.
2. Anticipation and fulfillment of each guest's needs.
3. A fond farewell, using the guest's name.

The Employee Promise

The Employee Promise underscores the company's commitment to its staff. It assures employees that they will be treated with respect, their opinions will be valued, and they will be given the tools and opportunities to grow both personally and professionally.

Strategies for Cultivating Appreciation and Recognition

The Ritz-Carlton employs a variety of strategies to cultivate a culture of appreciation and recognition. These strategies ensure that employees feel valued, motivated, and empowered to deliver exceptional service.

Daily Line-Ups

One of the most distinctive practices at the Ritz-Carlton is the daily line-up. Every day, employees across all departments gather for a brief meeting where they share stories of exceptional service, discuss the company's Gold Standards, and recognize colleagues who have gone above and beyond. This daily ritual reinforces the company's values, fosters a sense of community, and keeps employees aligned with the mission of providing outstanding service.

Employee Empowerment

The Ritz-Carlton empowers its employees to make decisions that enhance guest satisfaction. Staff members are authorized to spend up to $2,000 per guest, per incident, without needing management approval, to resolve issues or create memorable experiences. This level of trust and empowerment demonstrates the company's appreciation for its employees' judgment and dedication.

Five-Star Awards

The Ritz-Carlton's Five-Star Award program recognizes employees who consistently demonstrate exceptional performance and embody the company's Gold Standards. Recipients of this prestigious award receive a pin, a certificate, and public recognition during the daily line-up. This program not only rewards high achievers but also sets a benchmark for excellence within the organization.

Length of Service Awards

To honor the loyalty and dedication of long-serving employees, the Ritz-Carlton offers Length of Service Awards. These awards recognize employees for their years of service with the company, starting at five years and continuing in five-year increments. The awards often include a certificate, a gift, and a special ceremony, reinforcing the company's appreciation for long-term commitment.

Personalized Recognition

The Ritz-Carlton understands the importance of personalized recognition. Managers are encouraged to learn about their employees' interests and preferences so that they can provide meaningful and personalized acknowledgments. Whether it's a handwritten note, a favorite treat, or a small gift, these gestures go a long way in making employees feel valued and appreciated.

Impact on Employees and Guests

The culture of appreciation and recognition at the Ritz-Carlton has a profound impact on both employees and guests.

Employee Engagement and Satisfaction

Employees who feel appreciated and recognized are more likely to be engaged, motivated, and loyal. The Ritz-Carlton's commitment to creating a positive work environment ensures that staff members are happy and satisfied, which in turn translates to exceptional service for guests. High levels of employee engagement also lead to lower turnover rates and a strong sense of community within the company.

Exceptional Guest Experiences

A motivated and empowered workforce is essential to delivering the legendary service that the Ritz-Carlton is known for. Guests consistently experience personalized, attentive, and memorable service, which enhances their overall satisfaction and loyalty to the brand. The culture of appreciation and recognition ensures that employees are not only willing but eager to go above and beyond for guests.

Building a Strong Brand Reputation

The Ritz-Carlton's commitment to appreciation and recognition contributes to its stellar reputation as a leading luxury hotel brand. By consistently delivering exceptional service and creating memorable experiences for guests, the company strengthens its brand and maintains its position at the forefront of the hospitality industry.

The Ritz-Carlton Hotel Company's culture of appreciation and recognition is a cornerstone of its success. By valuing and empowering its employees, the company creates an environment where exceptional service and guest satisfaction are the norms. The Gold Standards, daily line-ups, and various recognition programs all contribute to a workplace culture that celebrates excellence and fosters a sense of belonging and pride among employees. As a result, the Ritz-Carlton continues to set the benchmark for luxury hospitality, inspiring both its employees and its guests to achieve greatness.

Conclusion: Honoring Leadership for a Better Future

Honoring leaders is not just about showing respect; it is about fostering a culture of gratitude, learning, and support. By acknowledging their contributions, showing respect and gratitude, learning from their example, supporting their vision, providing constructive feedback, celebrating their successes, supporting their well-being, and building a culture of appreciation, we create an environment where effective leadership can thrive.

When you meet leaders, take the time to honor them thoughtfully and sincerely. Your actions not only affirm their efforts but also inspire others to value and pursue effective leadership. In doing so, you contribute to a more respectful, motivated, and visionary society.

Chapter- 6

Wise to be Away from the Foolish

Throughout life, we encounter a variety of individuals, each with their own characteristics and behaviors. While it's important to show compassion and understanding, it's equally vital to recognize when associating with certain people can be detrimental. This chapter explores the importance of avoiding foolish people to guide you in making wise choices about your associations.

In the spring of 2018, Rohan was at a peak in his professional and personal life. His career was thriving, his creative projects were receiving recognition, and he felt surrounded by supportive friends and family. Among these friends was Alex, a charismatic and ambitious individual who had been a constant companion during these good times.

Rohan and Alex shared many intellectual conversations, exchanged ideas, and supported each other's endeavors. Their bond seemed strong, and Rohan valued Alex's friendship immensely. However, as time passed, Rohan began to notice unsettling traits in Alex's behavior. His ego grew with his achievements, and he often displayed a sense of superiority, dismissing others' contributions and efforts, including Rohan's.

Despite Rohan's success and the recognition he was receiving for his creative work, Alex rarely offered genuine praise. Instead, he would make subtle remarks that belittled Rohan's accomplishments, and his jealousy became increasingly apparent. What was once a supportive friendship started to feel like a one-sided competition, with Alex constantly trying to assert his dominance.

The turning point came when Rohan confided in Alex about a new, ambitious project he was working on. Excited about the potential impact, Rohan shared his ideas and plans in detail, trusting Alex as a close friend. To Rohan's dismay, Alex began to use this information against him. He would subtly undermine Rohan's efforts in front of others, questioning his abilities and spreading doubt about the project's feasibility.

It wasn't long before Alex's true intentions surfaced. He started to share Rohan's confidential thoughts and plans with others, twisting the narrative to paint Rohan in a negative light. He would bring up their personal conversations in public forums, often distorting the facts to embarrass Rohan or cast doubt on his integrity. This behavior was a stark contrast to the supportive friend Rohan once knew, and it became clear that Alex's actions were driven by jealousy and insecurity.

Rohan realized that Alex's foolish behavior was rooted in his inability to celebrate others' successes and his need to feel superior. Recognizing the wisdom in distancing himself from such negativity, Rohan made a conscious decision to step back from the friendship. It wasn't easy to part ways with someone who had once been so meaningful, but Rohan understood that Alex's toxic behavior was draining his energy and affecting his well-being.

By choosing to walk away, Rohan demonstrated wisdom in prioritizing his mental health and personal growth. He began to focus on nurturing relationships with individuals who genuinely supported and celebrated his successes. In the aftermath of distancing himself from Alex, Rohan found a renewed sense of peace and clarity. Without the constant negativity and undermining, Rohan was able to channel his energy into his creative projects and personal development.

The experience taught Rohan invaluable lessons about the importance of choosing friends who uplift and inspire, rather than those who seek to tear you down. By making a wise choice to avoid foolish behavior, Rohan paved the way for a more fulfilling and harmonious life.

Life Lessons from the Experience with Alex

1. Recognize Red Flags: Pay attention to signs of jealousy, ego, and manipulative behavior. These red flags often indicate deeper issues that can lead to toxic dynamics.

2. Value Genuine Support: Seek out friendships with people who genuinely celebrate your successes and offer constructive feedback. Genuine support fosters mutual growth and positivity.

3. Trust Your Instincts: If you feel uncomfortable or sense that someone is undermining you, trust your instincts and take steps to protect yourself.

4. Communicate Boundaries: Clearly define and communicate your boundaries. Protect your personal and professional information from those who may misuse it.

5. Reflect on Relationships: Regularly evaluate your relationships and their impact on your life. Make conscious decisions to distance yourself from those who bring negativity or harm.

Strategies for Avoiding Foolish People

In treasuring humility and avoiding foolishness, we cultivate an environment that fosters growth, wisdom, and genuine connection. By making conscious decisions about the company we keep, we ensure that our lives are enriched by positive influences, paving the way for a fulfilling and harmonious existence.

Understanding Foolishness

"Fools rush in where angels fear to tread."

- Alexander Pope

Foolishness is often characterized by a lack of good judgment, disregard for consequences, and a tendency to make irresponsible decisions. While everyone makes mistakes, consistently foolish behavior can lead to negative outcomes for those involved. Understanding these traits helps us identify when it's best to distance ourselves from such individuals.

The Impact of Foolish Associations

"Walk with the wise and become wise, for a companion of fools suffers harm."

- Proverbs 13:20

Associating with foolish people can have significant adverse effects on your life. Their poor judgment and reckless behavior can influence your decisions, lead to unnecessary conflicts, and create stressful situations. Protecting yourself from these negative influences is crucial for maintaining your well-being and achieving your goals.

The Rise and Fall of Enron : A Cautionary Tale

The story of Enron is one of the most infamous cases of corporate fraud and collapse in American history. Once a symbol of innovation and success, Enron's spectacular rise and even more dramatic fall serve as a powerful cautionary tale about the dangers of corporate greed, unethical behavior, and the importance of transparency and accountability in business practices.

The Rise of Enron Enron was founded in 1985 as a merger between Houston Natural Gas and Inter North, a Nebraska-based natural gas company. Under the leadership of Kenneth Lay, Enron quickly transformed from a traditional energy company into a diversified energy trading firm. By the 1990s, Enron had expanded into various sectors, including electricity, broadband services, and even weather derivatives. The company was lauded for its innovative business model and was consistently ranked among the most admired companies in America.

Key Factors in Enron's Rise

1. Innovation in Energy Trading: Enron pioneered the trading of energy contracts, which allowed the company to capitalize on the deregulation of the energy markets. This innovation provided a significant boost to their revenue and market influence.

2. Charismatic Leadership: Kenneth Lay, along with Jeffrey Skilling, who joined Enron in 1990, were seen as visionary leaders who could navigate the complexities of the evolving energy markets. Skilling's advocacy for a performance review system, known as "rank and yank," created a competitive and aggressive corporate culture.

3. Rapid Expansion: Enron's aggressive growth strategy included international ventures and diversification into various industries. The company's willingness to take risks and invest in new technologies kept it at the forefront of the market.

The Fall of Enron Despite its outward success, Enron's foundation was built on a series of unethical and illegal practices. The company's downfall began to unfold in 2001, revealing a web of financial manipulations designed to hide debt and inflate profits.

Key Factors in Enron's Fall

1. Accounting Fraud: Enron used complex financial structures and special purpose entities (SPEs) to keep debt off its balance sheet. These SPEs were used to hide losses and fabricate profits, creating a misleading picture of the company's financial health.

2. Corporate Malfeasance: Executives engaged in insider trading, selling their stock while publicly promoting the company's stability. They also pressured auditors and investment banks to overlook or support their fraudulent activities.

3. Lack of Oversight: Arthur Andersen, Enron's auditing firm, failed to provide the necessary oversight. The auditors were complicit in the fraud, and their role in the scandal led to the firm's eventual dissolution.

4. Market Manipulation: Enron manipulated energy markets, particularly in California, to create artificial shortages and inflate prices. This unethical behavior not only harmed consumers but also attracted regulatory scrutiny.

The Unraveling In August 2001, Jeffrey Skilling abruptly resigned as CEO, citing personal reasons. This move raised suspicions and triggered a deeper investigation into Enron's financial practices. In October 2001, Enron announced it was restating its earnings for the past four years, effectively admitting to inflating profits by nearly $600 million. The final blow came in December 2001, when Enron filed for bankruptcy. The collapse wiped out thousands of jobs, billions of dollars in shareholder value, and significantly damaged the reputation of corporate America.

The Aftermath The Enron scandal had far-reaching consequences. Several top executives, including Kenneth Lay and Jeffrey Skilling, were convicted of fraud and other crimes. Lay passed away before serving his sentence, while Skilling served more than 12 years in prison. The scandal led to the creation of the Sarbanes-Oxley Act of 2002, which aimed to protect investors by improving the accuracy and reliability of corporate disclosures. The Act introduced stricter regulations for public companies and established greater accountability for executives and auditors.

Lessons Learned The Enron debacle offers several critical lessons for businesses and regulators alike:

1. Importance of Transparency: Companies must maintain transparency in their financial reporting and business practices to build trust with investors, employees, and the public.

2. Ethical Leadership: Leaders must prioritize ethical behavior and foster a corporate culture that values integrity over short-term gains.

3. Regulatory Oversight: Robust regulatory frameworks are essential to prevent corporate fraud and protect the interests of stakeholders.

4. Corporate Accountability: Executives and auditors must be held accountable for their actions to ensure that unethical behavior is met with appropriate consequences.

The story of Enron is a stark reminder of the catastrophic consequences that can arise from corporate greed and unethical behavior. While Enron's rise was meteoric, its fall was a powerful testament to the importance of transparency, accountability, and ethical leadership in business. As we reflect on Enron's legacy, it is crucial to remember these lessons and strive to build a corporate world that prioritizes integrity and trust.

Recognizing Foolish Behavior

"Wise men learn more from fools than fools from the wise."

- Cato the Elder

Recognizing foolish behavior is the first step in avoiding it. Look for patterns of irresponsibility, dishonesty, and a disregard for the well-being of others. Foolish people often fail to learn from their mistakes, repeat poor decisions, and may exhibit arrogance or an unwillingness to listen to advice.

In literature, Shakespeare's character Falstaff from "Henry IV" embodies foolishness with his cowardice, gluttony, and disregard for honor. His behavior serves as a cautionary tale about the consequences of aligning oneself with foolish individuals.

Maintaining Boundaries

"You are the average of the five people you spend the most time with."

- Jim Rohn

Establishing and maintaining boundaries is essential when dealing with foolish people. Politely but firmly limit your interactions with them, especially in situations where their influence might impact your decisions or reputation. Protect your mental and emotional space by surrounding yourself with individuals who exhibit wisdom and integrity.

In the corporate world, successful leaders often attribute their achievements to maintaining a network of supportive and wise advisors, rather than engaging with those who might derail their focus and goals.

Learning from Their Mistakes

"The only real mistake is the one from which we learn nothing."

- Henry Ford

While it's crucial to avoid foolish people, there's value in observing and learning from their mistakes. Understanding the consequences of their actions can reinforce your own commitment to making wiser choices. Reflect on their failures to reinforce your understanding of good judgment and decision-making.

The Story of Icarus: A Greek Mythology Tale

The myth of Icarus is one of the most famous stories from Greek mythology, embodying themes of ambition, hubris, and the consequences of overreaching one's limits. It tells the tale of a young man whose daring flight with wings made of feathers and wax ultimately leads to his tragic downfall. This story has been retold through generations, serving as a timeless lesson about the dangers of hubris and the importance of heeding wisdom.

The Birth of Icarus

Icarus was the son of Daedalus, a master craftsman and inventor who served King Minos of Crete. Daedalus was renowned for his ingenuity and skill, and his creations were highly prized. However, despite his talents, Daedalus found himself entangled in the dangerous and treacherous politics of the Cretan court.

The Labyrinth and the Minotaur

King Minos commissioned Daedalus to construct a labyrinth, a vast and complex maze, to imprison the Minotaur, a monstrous creature that was half-man, half-bull. The labyrinth was so intricately designed that even Daedalus himself had difficulty navigating it. The Minotaur was kept in the center of the labyrinth, and each year, Athens was forced to send seven young men and seven young women as a tribute to be devoured by the beast.

Daedalus and Icarus Imprisoned

Eventually, Daedalus fell out of favor with King Minos. The reasons for this vary in different versions of the myth, but one common element is that Daedalus helped Theseus, a prince of Athens, navigate the labyrinth and defeat the Minotaur with the aid of Minos' daughter, Ariadne. Enraged by this betrayal, King Minos imprisoned Daedalus and his son Icarus in a high tower, preventing them from escaping the island of Crete by land or sea.

The Invention of the Wings

Determined to escape, Daedalus conceived a daring plan. Observing the birds flying freely in the sky, he decided to create wings for himself and Icarus. Using feathers collected from birds, Daedalus fashioned the wings and bound them together with thread and wax. He carefully instructed Icarus on how to use the wings, warning him of the dangers of flying too high or too low. If Icarus flew too low, the sea's moisture would weigh down the wings; if he flew too high, the sun's heat would melt the wax.

The Flight

With the wings secured to their bodies, Daedalus and Icarus leaped from the tower and soared into the sky. The sensation of flight was exhilarating, and for a time, it seemed that their escape would be successful. As they flew over the sea, the island of Crete became a distant memory, and Icarus, intoxicated by the freedom of flight, began to climb higher and higher, forgetting his father's warnings.

The Fall of Icarus

Overcome with the thrill of flight and his newfound freedom, Icarus soared towards the sun, ignoring Daedalus' desperate pleas to stay on course. As he ascended, the heat of the sun began to soften the wax that held his wings together. Soon, the feathers started to detach, and Icarus realized too late the peril of his ambition. His wings disintegrated, and he plummeted into the sea below. The waters where he fell were later named the Icarian Sea in his memory, and the nearby island was called Icaria.

The Aftermath

Daedalus, heartbroken by the loss of his son, continued his journey and eventually found refuge in Sicily. There, he sought the protection of King Cocalus and continued his work as a craftsman. Daedalus' grief over Icarus' death was profound, and he dedicated much of his remaining life to mourning his son and reflecting on the events that led to their tragic escape.

Themes and Lessons

The myth of Icarus offers several powerful themes and lessons:

1. The Dangers of Hubris: Icarus' overconfidence and disregard for his father's warnings illustrate the consequences of hubris, or excessive pride. His ambition to reach the heavens led to his downfall, serving as a reminder to respect one's limitations.

2. The Importance of Heeding Wisdom: Daedalus' warnings were based on experience and careful thought. Icarus' failure to heed his father's advice highlights the importance of listening to wisdom and guidance from those more experienced.

3. The Balance Between Ambition and Caution: The story emphasizes the need for balance between striving for greatness and exercising caution. While ambition can drive progress and achievement, it must be tempered with awareness of potential risks.

4. The Unpredictability of Fate: Despite careful planning and ingenuity, Daedalus could not foresee every variable in their escape. This aspect of the myth underscores the unpredictable nature of life and the role of fate in human endeavors.

The story of Icarus remains a poignant and enduring myth in Greek mythology. It captures the complexities of human ambition and the delicate balance between aspiration and prudence. Through the tale of Icarus' tragic flight, we are reminded of the timeless lessons about the consequences of over reaching and the importance of humility and wisdom.

The story of Icarus from Greek mythology, who foolishly flew too close to the sun despite warnings, teaches a valuable lesson about the dangers of hubris and ignoring sound advice.

Practicing Empathy Without Engagement

"Do not answer a fool according to his folly, or you yourself will be just like him."

- Proverbs 26:4

While it's important to avoid engaging with foolish behavior, practicing empathy is also essential. Recognize that everyone has their own journey and struggles. Offer kindness and support from a distance, but do not allow yourself to be drawn into their patterns of poor decision-making.

In social settings, it's possible to show compassion to someone who consistently makes poor choices without becoming involved in their dramas. Offering advice or support without entangling yourself in their issues demonstrates empathy while maintaining your boundaries.

Choosing Wise Associations

"Surround yourself with only people who are going to lift you higher."

- Oprah Winfrey

Actively seek out and cultivate relationships with wise, responsible individuals. These associations can inspire you, provide valuable guidance, and contribute positively to your personal and professional growth. Prioritize connections with those who exhibit good judgment, integrity, and a positive outlook.

The Friendship Between Bill Gates and Warren Buffett: A Testament to Wise Association and Mutual Benefit

The friendship between Bill Gates and Warren Buffett is one of the most remarkable partnerships in modern history. As two of the wealthiest and most influential individuals in the world, their relationship transcends mere business interests. It is a profound example of how wise associations can lead to mutual benefits, personal growth, and significant positive impacts on society.

The Beginnings of a Remarkable Friendship

Bill Gates, the co-founder of Microsoft, and Warren Buffett, the chairman and CEO of Berkshire Hathaway, first met in 1991. Despite initial reservations—Gates famously thought he had little in common with Buffett—their meeting turned into a deep and lasting friendship. The connection between the two men was immediate, marked by shared values, mutual respect, and a common vision for using their resources to improve the world.

Shared Values and Interests

Both Gates and Buffett are known for their intellectual curiosity, passion for learning, and commitment to philanthropy. These shared values formed the foundation of their friendship. They quickly found common ground in their discussions about business, investments, and life philosophies, often engaging in long conversations that delved into a wide range of topics.

Mutual Benefits of Their Association

The friendship between Gates and Buffett has been mutually beneficial in several profound ways. Their association has not only enriched their personal lives but also had a significant impact on their professional endeavors and philanthropic efforts.

Intellectual Exchange and Growth

One of the key benefits of their friendship is the intellectual exchange and growth it fosters. Gates and Buffett regularly share ideas, challenge each other's thinking, and provide valuable insights. This exchange of knowledge and perspectives has helped both men expand their understanding and approach to various aspects of business and life.

Gates, known for his deep knowledge of technology and innovation, has gained a more nuanced understanding of value investing from Buffett. Conversely, Buffett has benefited from Gates' insights into technological advancements and their potential impacts on the future of business.

Philanthropic Collaboration

Perhaps the most significant outcome of their friendship is their collaboration in philanthropy. In 2006, Buffett announced that he would donate the majority of his fortune to the Bill & Melinda Gates Foundation. This unprecedented act of generosity solidified their partnership in tackling some of the world's most pressing issues, including global health, education, and poverty alleviation.

The Giving Pledge: In 2010, Gates and Buffett co-founded The Giving Pledge, an initiative that encourages the world's wealthiest individuals to commit to giving the majority of their wealth to philanthropic causes. This initiative has inspired many other billionaires to join the cause, amplifying the impact of their philanthropic efforts.

Personal Growth and Support

Beyond their professional and philanthropic collaborations, Gates and Buffett have supported each other through personal challenges and milestones. Their friendship has provided both men with a source of personal growth, emotional support, and inspiration.

Gates often speaks about how Buffett's wisdom and life philosophy have influenced his own approach to business and personal life. Buffett's emphasis on finding joy in simple pleasures, maintaining humility, and prioritizing meaningful relationships has resonated deeply with Gates.

Lessons from Their Friendship

The friendship between Gates and Buffett offers several valuable lessons about the importance and benefits of wise associations:

1. **Surround Yourself with Like-Minded Individuals**

   Gates and Buffett's friendship illustrates the importance of surrounding oneself with like-minded individuals who share similar values and goals. By doing so, one can create an environment that fosters mutual growth, support, and inspiration.

2. **Value Intellectual Exchange**

   Engaging in meaningful conversations and exchanging ideas with others can lead to significant intellectual growth. Gates and Buffett's regular discussions have helped both men expand their knowledge and refine their perspectives.

3. Collaborate for Greater Impact

Their partnership in philanthropy demonstrates the power of collaboration in achieving greater impact. By combining their resources and expertise, Gates and Buffett have been able to tackle global challenges more effectively than they could have individually.

4. Prioritize Personal Growth and Relationships

Their friendship highlights the importance of personal growth and the value of meaningful relationships. Gates and Buffett have supported each other through various life stages, providing emotional support and inspiration along the way.

The friendship between Bill Gates and Warren Buffett is a shining example of the benefits of wise associations. Through their shared values, intellectual exchange, and collaborative efforts, they have enriched each other's lives and made significant contributions to society. Their relationship serves as a powerful reminder of the importance of surrounding oneself with like-minded individuals, valuing intellectual growth, collaborating for greater impact, and prioritizing personal growth and meaningful relationships. As Gates and Buffett continue to inspire each other and the world, their friendship stands as a testament to the profound impact of wise associations.

Setting an Example

"The best way to teach others is to lead by example."

- Unknown

By living with integrity and making wise choices, you set a positive example for others, including those who may exhibit foolish behavior. Your actions can inspire change and encourage others to adopt more responsible behaviors. Leading by example is a powerful way to influence those around you positively.

Nelson Mandela's leadership and unwavering commitment to justice and reconciliation set a powerful example for others, transforming not only individuals but an entire nation. His leadership is widely admired for its courage, resilience, and commitment to reconciliation. As the first black president of South Africa, he played a crucial role in dismantling apartheid and promoting social justice. Mandela's leadership style was characterised by inclusivity, forgiveness, and a vision of a unified nation. He emphasized dialogue over conflict, exemplifying the power of forgiveness and recociliationin fostering national unity. His ability to inspire and lead through adversity continues to be a powerful example worldwide.

Conclusion: Navigating Life with Wisdom

Avoiding foolish people is not about judgment or exclusion; it's about making wise choices to protect your well-being and future. By recognizing foolish behavior, maintaining boundaries, learning from others' mistakes, practicing empathy without engagement, choosing wise associations, and setting a positive example, you navigate life with greater wisdom and integrity.

In doing so, you not only safeguard your own path but also contribute to a culture of responsibility and good judgment. Embrace the journey of discernment, and let your choices reflect the wisdom you seek to embody.

Chapter- 7

Treasuring Humility from the Humble

In a world often driven by ambition and self-promotion, encountering humble individuals can be a refreshing and enlightening experience. Humble people possess a quiet strength and a genuine concern for others that make them invaluable in our lives. This chapter explores the importance of treasuring humble people to guide you in recognizing and appreciating the virtues of humility.

In the summer of 2019, Father Norbert found himself strolling through the bustling streets of Kolkta's NSC Bose Road, India. His purpose was twofold: to explore the rich cultural tapestry of the city and to conduct research for my upcoming book on human connections. Little did he knew, this journey would introduce him to an extraordinary individual whose humility would leave a lasting impact in his life.

That sweltering afternoon, Father Norbert decided to visit a local market known for its vibrant array of goods and lively atmosphere. As he navigated through the crowded lanes, his attention was drawn to a small saloon nestled between towering buildings. The saloon, adorned with colorful garlands and a modest sign reading "Raj's Hair Saloon," exuded an inviting charm. Father Norbert approached, eager to dress his hair and perhaps learn more about the people who frequented this quaint establishment.

Behind the hair cut chair stood Raj, a man in his mid-50s with a warm smile and eyes that radiated kindness. His attire was simple—worn-out clothes that spoke of a life of hard work and dedication. Despite the bustling environment, Raj seemed to exude a sense of calm and contentment that piqued my curiosity.

As Raj began dressing Father Norbert's hair, he struck up a conversation with Raj. He shared that he had been running the saloon for over two decades. What fascinated Father Norbert most was not his entrepreneurial spirit, but his genuine concern for the people in his community. Raj recounted how he had started the saloon first on the foot path with the intention of providing affordable, quality hair dressing to the working-class individuals who frequented the area.

Over the years, Raj's humble saloon had become a sanctuary for many—a place where people could gather, share their stories, and find solace in each other's company. Raj's unwavering humility and generosity had earned him the respect and admiration of everyone who crossed his path. He never sought recognition or accolades; instead, he found joy in serving others and making a positive impact on their lives.

One story in particular stood out. Raj told Father Norbert about a young boy named Aarav who had lost his parents at a tender age and was struggling to make ends meet. Raj had taken Aarav under his wing, providing him with meals, school supplies, and emotional support. Today, Aarav was a successful engineer, and he often visited Raj to express his gratitude.

As the conversation deepened, Father Norbert realized that Raj's humility was not just a trait but a way of life. He approached each day with a selfless attitude, finding fulfillment in the happiness and well-being of others. His hair dressing in the saloon was not just a business; it was a testament to the power of humility and the profound impact one person could have on an entire community.

Raj's story left an indelible mark on Father Norbert. It reminded him that true strength lies in humility and that genuine concern for others can create ripples of positive change. In a world where ambition and self-promotion often take center stage, Raj's humble spirit shone as a beacon of hope and inspiration.

Life Lessons from Raj's Humility

1. The Power of Selflessness:

Raj's story illustrates that true fulfillment comes from serving others. By prioritizing the needs of his community over personal gain, Raj created a space of warmth and support that transformed countless lives.

2. Strength in Humility:

Humility is not a sign of weakness but a testament to inner strength. Raj's humble demeanor allowed him to connect with people on a deeper level, fostering trust and respect.

3. Creating Positive Change:

One person's humble actions can create a ripple effect of positive change. Raj's generosity and kindness inspired others to pay it forward, building a stronger, more compassionate community.

4. Finding Joy in Simplicity:

Raj found joy in the simple act of making tea and serving his customers. This teaches us to appreciate the small, everyday moments and find contentment in the present.

5. The Lasting Impact of Kindness:

Acts of humility and kindness have a lasting impact. Raj's support for Aarav not only changed the boy's life but also left a legacy of gratitude and inspiration.

Strategies to Recognize and Appreciate Humility

In treasuring humility, we learn to see the world through a lens of compassion and selflessness. Humble individuals like Raj remind us that true greatness lies not in wealth or status but in the quiet strength of a generous heart. By recognizing and appreciating the virtues of humility, we enrich our own lives and create a more compassionate and connected world.

The Beauty of Humility

"Humility is not thinking less of yourself, it's thinking of yourself less."

- C.S. Lewis

Humility is a quality that involves recognizing one's limitations, valuing others, and seeking to serve rather than dominate. Humble people do not seek the limelight; instead, they focus on contributing positively to those around them. Their selflessness and modesty create an environment of trust and respect.

Recognizing Humility in Others

"True humility is staying teachable, regardless of how much you already know."

- Unknown

Recognizing humility involves looking beyond outward appearances and achievements. Humble people often listen more than they speak, show gratitude for the contributions of others, and admit when they are wrong. They inspire others through their actions rather than their words.

Nelson Mandela, despite his monumental achievements, remained humble throughout his life. He acknowledged the contributions of his comrades in the struggle against apartheid and often deflected praise to highlight the collective effort.

Valuing Their Contributions

"No one is useless in this world who lightens the burdens of another."

- Charles Dickens

Humble individuals often make significant contributions without seeking recognition. Valuing their efforts involves acknowledging their work, expressing gratitude, and ensuring their contributions are not overlooked. This recognition can motivate them and others to continue their selfless efforts.

In the healthcare sector, many nurses and support staff work tirelessly behind the scenes. Their humble service is crucial for patient care, and recognizing their efforts through appreciation and awards highlights the importance of their contributions.

In a bustling hospital, Nurse Maria was known for her unwavering dedication to patient care. One evening, she was assigned to care for Mr. Johnson, an elderly man recovering from surgery. Despite the chaos of the ward, Maria always found time to sit with Mr. Johnson, listening attentively to his concerns and offering gentle reassurances.

One particularly busy night, Mr. Johnson was feeling anxious and restless. Maria noticed his discomfort and took extra care to ensure he was comfortable. She stayed by his side, holding his hand and talking to him soothingly. When he mentioned missing his wife, who couldn't visit due to the late hour, Maria took the time to share stories about her own family, creating a sense of warmth and familiarity.

As the night wore on, Maria noticed Mr. Johnson becoming increasingly fatigued. She anticipated his needs before he even voiced them—adjusting his pillows, fetching water, and ensuring his pain was managed effectively. Despite the demands of her shift, Maria never rushed through her interactions with Mr. Johnson, always maintaining a calm and compassionate demeanor.

In the early hours of the morning, Mr. Johnson finally drifted off to sleep, comforted by Maria's presence and care. Reflecting on her shift later, Maria didn't seek recognition or praise for her efforts. For her, providing compassionate care was simply part of her commitment to every patient's well-being.

This story illustrates how nurses, like Maria, embody humility and dedication in their service to patients, going above and beyond to ensure comfort and emotional support during challenging times.

Learning from Their Example

"The highest form of wisdom is humility."

- Talmud

Humble people provide powerful lessons in modesty, self-awareness, and compassion. Observing their behavior can inspire you to adopt these qualities in your own life. Reflect on how they handle success and failure, interact with others, and approach their responsibilities.

Mother Teresa, known for her profound humility, dedicated her life to serving the poorest of the poor in Calcutta, India, and around the world. Born Agnes Gonxha Bojaxhiu in 1910 in Skopje, Macedonia, she felt a calling to religious life from an early age. At the age of 18, she joined the Sisters of Loreto, where she took the name Sister Teresa.

In 1946, while traveling by train to Darjeeling for a retreat, Sister Teresa experienced what she described as a "call within a call." She felt compelled to leave the convent and work directly with the poorest and most neglected people in the slums of Calcutta. With permission from the Church and against considerable resistance and skepticism, she set out to start her mission of love and care.

Mother Teresa began her work by providing basic medical care, establishing schools, and offering food and shelter to those in need. She and her fellow sisters lived among the poor, sharing in their hardships and serving them with deep compassion. Mother Teresa's approach was deeply rooted in humility and a belief in the dignity of every human being, regardless of their circumstances or background.

Despite facing numerous challenges and often operating with limited resources, Mother Teresa remained steadfast in her commitment to serve. Her humility was evident in her simple lifestyle, characterized by personal austerity and a focus on the needs of others above her own. She saw herself not as a hero but as a servant of God, fulfilling what she believed was her life's purpose.

Throughout her life, Mother Teresa received international recognition for her humanitarian work, including the Nobel Peace Prize in 1979. However, she continued to live a life of humility, deflecting personal praise and always redirecting attention to the plight of the poor. Her legacy continues to inspire people worldwide to embrace humility, compassion, and selfless service in their own lives.

Mother Teresa's life is a testament to humility. Her dedication to serving the poorest of the poor, without seeking fame or reward, provides a profound example of living a life of humility and service.

Supporting Their Efforts

"The greatest among you will be your servant."

- Matthew 23:11

Support the efforts of humble individuals by offering your help and resources. Whether it's volunteering for their initiatives, providing financial support, or simply offering encouragement, your support can amplify their impact and show that their humility is valued.

In a small town called Riverside, a group of local community leaders noticed the increasing struggles of families due to economic hardships. Unemployment rates were high, and many families were finding it difficult to put food on the table. Recognizing the urgent need, these leaders decided to take action.

The group, led by Mayor Laura, Pastor Mike, and Principal Emma, came together to form the Riverside Care Coalition. Their mission was to provide support to families in need and foster a sense of unity within the community. They began by organizing a weekly food drive, reaching out to local businesses, farms, and residents for donations.

Mayor Laura used her connections to secure contributions from local supermarkets and food suppliers. She also volunteered her weekends to help sort and distribute food packages. Pastor Mike rallied his congregation, encouraging them to donate non-perishable items and volunteer their time. He often spent his evenings driving the church van to deliver food to those who couldn't make it to the distribution center.

Principal Emma, seeing the impact on her students, organized school-wide events to collect donations and raise awareness. She encouraged students to participate, teaching them the value of giving back to their community. Emma spent countless hours after school organizing the donations and ensuring that families received what they needed.

The Riverside Care Coalition didn't stop at food distribution. They organized free tutoring sessions, job fairs, and health clinics, all staffed by volunteers from the community. Local doctors, teachers, and professionals donated their time and expertise to help their neighbors get back on their feet.

One winter, when a severe storm hit Riverside, many families found themselves without power and basic supplies. The Coalition quickly mobilized. Mayor Laura opened the town hall as a warming center and shelter, Pastor Mike coordinated a supply drive for blankets and warm clothing, and Principal Emma organized a team of volunteers to check on elderly residents and those with special needs.

The humble service of these community leaders had a profound impact. Their efforts not only provided immediate relief but also strengthened the bonds within the community. Families who once felt isolated and hopeless found support and a renewed sense of belonging.

The Riverside Care Coalition's work became a model for other towns facing similar challenges. Their story is a testament to the power of community leaders who, with humility and dedication, volunteer their time and resources to make a lasting difference in the lives of others.

This story highlights how the selfless efforts of community leaders can inspire collective action and bring about significant positive change.

Community leaders who work quietly to improve local conditions often need support to sustain their projects. By volunteering your time or donating resources, you help further their mission and demonstrate appreciation for their humble service.

Celebrating Their Achievements

> *"Humility is the solid foundation of all virtues."*
>
> *- Confucius*

While humble people may shy away from the spotlight, celebrating their achievements is important. It not only honors their hard work but also sets an example for others to emulate. Public recognition can inspire others to appreciate and practice humility.

Kailash Satyarthi, Nobel Peace Prize winner whose modesty and dedication to education have made a significant impact. Born on January 11, 1954, in Vidisha, India, Satyarthi is a tireless advocate for children's rights, particularly the right to education and freedom from child labor.

Early Life and Advocacy

Kailash Satyarthi began his career as an electrical engineer but soon shifted his focus to activism after witnessing the plight of child laborers. In 1980, he founded the Bachpan Bachao Andolan (Save Childhood Movement), which has since rescued over 100,000 children from slavery, trafficking, and exploitative labor.

Humble Beginnings

Satyarthi's approach has always been rooted in humility and grassroots activism. He personally led many raids on factories and workplaces where children were held in deplorable conditions, risking his life to free them. Despite the dangerous nature of his work, Satyarthi remained dedicated to his cause, often crediting the resilience and strength of the children he rescued as his source of inspiration.

Nobel Peace Prize and Continued Efforts

In 2014, Satyarthi was awarded the Nobel Peace Prize jointly with Malala Yousafzai. The Nobel Committee honored their efforts to combat the suppression of children and young people and to secure the right to education for all children. Satyarthi, in his acceptance speech, humbly dedicated the award to the children he worked for, stressing that it was a recognition of their suffering and courage.

Modesty and Dedication

Despite his global recognition, Satyarthi has remained remarkably modest. He continues to live a simple life, focusing on his mission rather than seeking personal accolades. His dedication to education and children's rights is evident in his ongoing work. He founded the Global March Against Child Labour, a movement that brought together millions of people across 103 countries to advocate for children's rights and education.

Impact and Legacy

Kailash Satyarthi's work has led to significant legislative and policy changes in India and internationally. His efforts contributed to the International Labour Organization (ILO) conventions on child labor and inspired the United Nations' Sustainable Development Goals, which include ending child labor by 2025.

His humility is reflected in his constant emphasis on collaboration and the collective effort required to address the complex issue of child labor. Satyarthi often highlights the contributions of his team and the bravery of the children he rescues, maintaining that true change comes from collective action and persistent effort.

Value of Humility

Satyarthi's life and work exemplify how humility can drive positive change. By focusing on the needs and voices of the most vulnerable, rather than seeking personal glory, he has been able to galvanize global support for children's rights. His modesty has allowed him to connect deeply with the communities he serves, making his advocacy both authentic and impactful.

Kailash Satyarthi's story is a powerful reminder that humility, coupled with unwavering dedication, can lead to profound and lasting change in the world.

The Nobel Peace Prize has been awarded to many humble leaders, such as Malala Yousafzai, whose modesty and dedication to education have made a significant impact. Celebrating such achievements highlights the value of humility in creating positive change.

Creating a Culture of Humility

"Humility is the true key to success."

- Rick Pitino

Fostering a culture that values humility involves encouraging behaviors that promote modesty, respect, and selflessness. Encourage open dialogue, appreciate the contributions of all team members, and create an environment where humility is recognized as a strength.

In workplaces, leaders can set an example by sharing credit, seeking feedback, and acknowledging their own mistakes. Such practices create a culture where humility is valued and emulated by others.

Susan, CEO of a Tech Startup

Susan, the CEO of a rapidly growing tech startup, is renowned for her leadership style that fosters a culture of humility and collaboration within her company.

Sharing Credit

Whenever her team achieves a significant milestone or successfully launches a new product, Susan is the first to highlight the contributions of her team members. In company meetings and public announcements, she ensures that the efforts of engineers, designers, marketers, and support staff are recognized. She frequently uses phrases like, "This achievement is a testament to the hard work and dedication of our entire team," and personally thanks individuals for their specific contributions.

Seeking Feedback

Susan actively seeks feedback from all levels of the organization. She holds regular "open door" sessions where employees can freely share their thoughts, ideas, and concerns. Additionally, she conducts anonymous surveys to gather honest opinions about the company's direction and her leadership. Susan acts on this feedback, implementing changes based on the team's input and showing that she values their perspectives.

Acknowledging Mistakes

During a critical project, Susan made a strategic decision that didn't yield the expected results. Instead of deflecting blame, she addressed the entire company, transparently explaining what went wrong and her role in the decision. She said, "I take full responsibility for the outcome of this project. Here's what I've learned, and here's how we're going to move forward." This acknowledgment not only built trust but also set a powerful example for her team.

Creating a Culture of Humility

Susan's actions have fostered a company culture where humility is valued and practiced. Employees feel comfortable admitting mistakes and learning from them, knowing that their leader does the same. Collaboration and open communication are cornerstones of the company's success, as team members feel respected and valued for their contributions.

Valued by Others

Susan's leadership has garnered immense respect and loyalty from her employees. Her willingness to share credit, seek feedback, and own up to her mistakes has created a positive, inclusive workplace environment. As a result, the company enjoys low turnover rates and high employee satisfaction. The culture of humility and mutual respect has also led to innovative ideas and solutions, driving the company's sustained growth and success.

Susan's leadership style exemplifies how humility can create a thriving workplace. By sharing credit, seeking feedback, and acknowledging mistakes, she has built a culture where employees feel valued and empowered, leading to a more cohesive and successful organization.

Practicing Gratitude

"Gratitude is the fairest blossom which springs from the soul."

- Henry Ward Beecher

Expressing gratitude to humble individuals reinforces their value and importance. Whether through verbal acknowledgment, written notes, or acts of kindness, showing gratitude strengthens bonds and encourages continued humility and service.

Writing a thank-you note to a humble mentor or colleague can have a profound impact. It shows that their quiet efforts are seen and appreciated, fostering a deeper sense of connection and mutual respect.

Reflecting on Personal Humility

> *"Humility is the mother of all virtues; purity, charity, and obedience. It is in being humble that our love becomes real, devoted, and ardent."*
>
> *- Mother Teresa*

Treasuring humble people also involves reflecting on your own humility. Consider how you can incorporate more humility into your life, whether through acts of service, seeking feedback, or recognizing the contributions of others. Personal growth in humility enhances your interactions and relationships.

Volunteering for community service, actively listening in conversations, and acknowledging the strengths of your peers are practical ways to cultivate and reflect on your own humility.

Conclusion: Embracing Humility

Treasuring humble people enriches our lives and communities. By recognizing and valuing their contributions, learning from their example, supporting their efforts, celebrating their achievements, creating a culture of humility, practicing gratitude, and reflecting on personal humility, we cultivate a deeper appreciation for this vital virtue.

Humility is a quiet strength that fosters genuine connections and meaningful contributions. Embrace the opportunity to learn from and honor humble individuals, and let their example inspire you to live with greater modesty, compassion, and integrity.

Chapter- 8

Better to Ignore the Arrogants

Arrogance is a trait characterized by an inflated sense of self-importance, a lack of humility, and a dismissive attitude towards others. Interacting with arrogant individuals can be challenging and draining, often leading to conflict and frustration.

One humid August evening, Father Norbert was at Kolkata's Netaji Bose airport, preparing for a flight to Mumbai. As Father Norbert boarded the Indigo flight, Norbert navigated through the narrow aisle to my seat, 9F. To Father Norbert's left in seat 9A, sat a man adorned in opulence-gold chains draped around his neck, a thick gold bracelet on his wrist, and a gleaming iPhone in hand. He exuded an air of arrogance, his eyes flickering disdainfully at anyone who glanced his way.

As the last few passengers trickled in, a heartwarming yet chaotic scene unfolded. Eight poor children, led by a compassionate woman likely from an NGO entered the plane. Their clothes were shabby, untidy, but they wore decent sandals looking as if purchased few hours ago and carried a mixture of excitement and nervousness on their faces. It seemed clear this was their first time on an airplane.

The children took their seats, filling the row that included the rich man in 9A. His face twisted with disgust, and he immediately summoned a flight attendant.

"I can't sit here with... with them!" he bellowed, pointing an accusatory finger at the children. "Move them or move me, but I will not share a row with these... street kids."

His voice cut through the cabin, drawing the attention of all the passengers. The flight attendants, caught in a difficult position, tried to soothe the situation.

"Sir, please calm down. These children have as much right to be here as you do," one attendant said, her tone firm yet polite.

"I paid for comfort, not for this! I demand to be moved now," the man insisted, his arrogance boiling over.

The other passengers, witnessing this display of rudeness, began to murmur in disapproval. A middle-aged woman across the aisle shook her head. A young man in the row behind them spoke up.

"Hey, buddy, why don't you move if you have such a problem? These kids are just excited to be here."

The rich man ignored the comments, maintaining his tirade against the children. The kids, visibly uncomfortable, huddled closer together, their initial excitement dimmed by the harsh encounter. The woman who had escorted them onto the flight did her best to reassure them, her calm demeanor a stark contrast to the rich man's fury.

Finally, after several tense minutes, the flight attendants managed to find new seats for the children. As they moved, the passengers erupted in applause, not for the resolution, but in solidarity with the children and the woman who cared for them. The rich man, however, remained impervious to the collective disapproval.

Throughout the flight, the atmosphere among the passengers remained supportive of the children. The flight attendants went out of their way to make the kids feel comfortable, offering extra snacks and engaging them in friendly conversation. The woman from the NGO received numerous compliments and words of encouragement from other passengers.

As Father Norbert sat quietly observing this unfold, Father Norbert couldn't help but reflect on the deeper lesson this experience provided. Arrogance, often rooted in a sense of superiority, can create unnecessary divisions and conflicts. Yet, in the face of such arrogance, the collective response of kindness and support can overpower negativity. The rich man, with all his wealth, displayed a poverty of spirit, while those children, despite their material lack, exuded a richness of potential and resilience.

The episode highlighted the importance of empathy and the power of community. It reminded me that every individual, regardless of their socio-economic status, deserves dignity and respect. The passengers' collective stance against arrogance served as a powerful testament to the human capacity for compassion and solidarity.

As the flight descended towards Mumbai, the children's smiles had returned, and the woman's dedication shone brighter than ever. This journey, initially marred by an unfortunate incident, became a narrative of unity and kindness—a reminder to always ignore arrogance and stand up for what is right.

The experience left an indelible mark on Father Norbert. It underscored the essence of human connection and the importance of fostering environments where everyone feels valued and respected. In a world often divided by class and privilege, moments like these illuminate the path to a more inclusive and

empathetic society.

Reflections and Life Lessons

1. Empathy Over Arrogance:

The incident on the flight showcased the importance of empathy. While the rich man displayed arrogance, the other passengers chose empathy, standing up for the children and making them feel welcome.

2. Power of Community:

The collective response of the passengers highlighted how powerful community support can be. When people unite against injustice, they can create a positive impact and uplift those who are marginalized.

3. Dignity and Respect:

Every individual deserves dignity and respect, regardless of their socioeconomic status. The children on the flight, though poor, were treated with kindness and compassion by the passengers and crew, reinforcing this fundamental human right.

4. Role of Compassionate Leadership:

The woman from the NGO demonstrated compassionate leadership. Her calm and caring demeanor provided comfort to the children and set an example for others on how to handle difficult situations with grace.

5. Personal Growth:

Witnessing this incident was a learning experience for me, emphasizing the importance of ignoring arrogance and choosing kindness. It reinforced the value of standing up for others and promoting a culture of empathy and respect.

By reflecting on this journey, we can draw valuable lessons that inspire us to foster human connections rooted in compassion and understanding, ultimately leading to a more inclusive and harmonious world.

Understanding Arrogance

"Arrogance is a creature. It does not have senses. It has only a sharp tongue and the pointing finger."

- Toba Beta

Arrogant individuals often exhibit a sense of superiority, belittling others and seeking validation for their own self-image. They may dismiss feedback, refuse to consider alternative viewpoints, and prioritize their own interests above all else. Recognizing these traits helps you navigate interactions with them more effectively.

The Pitfalls of Engaging with Arrogance

"An arrogant person considers himself perfect. This is the chief harm of arrogance. It interferes with a person's main task in life - becoming a better person."

- Leo Tolstoy

Engaging with arrogant people can be counterproductive, as it often leads to conflict and escalates tensions. Their unwillingness to listen or collaborate makes meaningful communication difficult, hindering progress and fostering resentment. Ignoring arrogance is often the best course of action to maintain your peace of mind and integrity.

The Problem

The marketing team at a mid-sized company was experiencing significant issues due to one colleague, Alex. Alex had a habit of dominating discussions, dismissing others' ideas, and constantly asserting that his approach was the best. This created a toxic atmosphere where team members felt undervalued and reluctant to share their ideas, stifling creativity and collaboration.

Addressing the Issue

1. Private Feedback Session: The team leader, Jenna, noticed the growing tension and decided to address the issue directly with Alex. In a private meeting, she provided constructive feedback, highlighting specific instances where Alex's behavior had been detrimental to team dynamics. She explained how his actions were affecting morale and productivity.

2. Team Workshop: Jenna organized a workshop focused on effective communication and teamwork. During the session, the team engaged in activities that emphasized the importance of listening, valuing diverse perspectives, and building on each other's ideas. The workshop also included role-playing exercises where team members practiced giving and receiving feedback in a constructive manner.

3. Establishing Ground Rules : The team collectively established ground rules for meetings to ensure everyone had an equal opportunity to contribute. These rules included:

- No interruptions while someone is speaking.

- Everyone gets a chance to share their ideas.

- Constructive feedback should be encouraged and welcomed.

4. Rotating Meeting Facilitators: To ensure balanced participation, the team decided to rotate the role of meeting facilitator among all members. The facilitator's job was to ensure the ground rules were followed and that everyone had a chance to contribute.

5. Regular Check-Ins : Jenna implemented regular check-ins with the team to discuss how the new measures were working and to address any ongoing issues. This allowed the team to continuously improve their collaboration process.

The Transformation

Over time, these interventions began to show positive results. Alex, though initially resistant, started to recognize the impact of his behavior and made efforts to adjust. The structured approach to meetings ensured that everyone's voice was heard, fostering a more inclusive environment.

Improved Atmosphere and Outcomes

- **Increased Creativity:** With a more open and respectful atmosphere, team members felt more comfortable sharing their ideas. This led to a surge in creativity, with more innovative campaigns and strategies being developed.

- **Enhanced Collaboration :** The team began to work more cohesively, leveraging each member's strengths and ideas. This improved the overall quality of their work and boosted team morale.

- **Personal Growth** : Alex learned valuable lessons in humility and the importance of collaboration. Over time, he became a more supportive and considerate team member, contributing to a healthier team dynamic.

This example illustrates how a team can effectively address the challenge of an arrogant colleague by providing constructive feedback, setting clear expectations, and fostering a culture of respect and collaboration. By taking these steps, the team was able to transform a toxic atmosphere into a productive and creative working environment.

Maintaining Your Composure

"Silence is the best reply to a fool."

- Imam Ali

Ignoring arrogance requires maintaining your composure and refusing to be drawn into unnecessary conflicts. Responding calmly and assertively, or choosing not to engage at all, demonstrates your strength and resilience in the face of provocation.

When confronted with arrogant behavior during a debate or negotiation, maintaining a composed demeanor and sticking to factual arguments can disarm the arrogant individual and prevent the situation from escalating into a heated confrontation.

Focusing on Your Goals

"Stay committed to your decisions, but stay flexible in your approach."

- Tony Robbins

When confronted with arrogance, it's important to stay focused on your goals and priorities. Refrain from getting sidetracked by the arrogant individual's attempts to undermine or distract you. Keep your eyes on the bigger picture and continue working towards your objectives.

In a professional setting, an arrogant boss may criticize your work unfairly or take credit for your achievements. By focusing on delivering high-quality results and maintaining a positive attitude, you demonstrate your professionalism and resilience despite the challenges.

Choosing Your Battles Wisely

"Sometimes it's best to stay silent. You can tell more about a person by what they don't say."

- Unknown

Not every instance of arrogance warrants a response. Assess the situation and choose your battles wisely. Consider whether engaging with the arrogant individual will lead to a productive outcome or if it's best to disengage and focus your energy elsewhere.

In social situations, encountering an arrogant acquaintance who constantly boasts about their achievements may tempt you to challenge them or compete for attention. However, recognizing that their behavior stems from insecurity, you may choose to avoid confrontation and interact with more humble individuals instead.

Seeking Support from Others

"There is no such thing as a 'self-made' person. We are made up of thousands of others."

- George Matthew Adams

Seeking support from others can provide validation and reassurance when dealing with arrogant individuals. Share your experiences with trusted friends, mentors, or colleagues who can offer perspective and guidance. Their empathy and insights can help you navigate challenging situations more effectively.

Discussing your interactions with an arrogant coworker with a supportive colleague can help you gain perspective and identify constructive ways to handle the situation. Their advice and encouragement empower you to maintain your confidence and integrity.

Setting Boundaries

"Respect yourself enough to walk away from anything that no longer serves you, grows you, or makes you happy."

- Unknown

Establishing clear boundaries with arrogant individuals is essential for maintaining your well-being and self-respect. Communicate assertively and diplomatically about what behavior is unacceptable to you, and be prepared to disengage if those boundaries are violated.

If a friend consistently belittles your achievements or disregards your feelings, assertively expressing your boundaries and refusing to tolerate disrespectful behavior sends a clear message that you prioritize mutual respect in your relationships.

Practicing Self-Reflection

"Knowing yourself is the beginning of all wisdom."

- Aristotle

Reflecting on your own reactions and triggers when faced with arrogance helps you develop self-awareness and emotional resilience. Identify patterns of behavior or thought that may contribute to escalating conflicts, and work on cultivating patience, empathy, and assertiveness in your interactions.

After a frustrating encounter with an arrogant coworker, take time to reflect on your emotional response and identify any underlying feelings of insecurity or frustration. Developing self-awareness allows you to respond more calmly and constructively in similar situations in the future.

Embracing Humility

"Humility is not thinking less of yourself, but thinking of yourself less."

- C.S. Lewis

Embracing humility in your interactions with arrogant individuals allows you to rise above their behavior and maintain your integrity. Focus on listening actively, acknowledging the perspectives of others, and treating everyone with respect, regardless of their demeanor.

Demonstrating humility in the face of arrogance involves resisting the temptation to retaliate or belittle the arrogant individual in return. Instead, approach the interaction with empathy and understanding, recognizing that their behavior may stem from insecurities or past experiences.

Conclusion: Choosing Grace over Conflict

Ignoring arrogance is not about weakness or submission; it's about choosing grace over conflict and prioritizing your own well-being and integrity. By maintaining your composure, focusing on your goals, choosing your battles wisely, seeking support from others, setting boundaries, practicing self-reflection, and embracing humility, you navigate interactions with arrogant individuals with dignity and resilience.

In doing so, you preserve your peace of mind and protect your relationships and reputation. Remember that you have the power to control your reactions and choices, and by ignoring arrogance, you maintain your autonomy and self-respect.

Chapter- 9

Being Closer to the Graceful

Gracious individuals possess a rare quality that sets them apart—whether through their kindness, generosity, or elegance in handling challenging situations. Their ability to navigate life with poise and compassion serves as a beacon of inspiration for those around them.

In the vibrant city of Joy, where the old and new blend seamlessly, Father Norbert had the privilege of crossing paths with an extraordinary individual, Mr. Nabarun De. As the respected Principal of Modern International Academy and a former executive member of the national educational board, Mr. De was a luminary in the field of education. His gracious demeanor and warm smiles left an indelible mark on everyone he encountered.

Father Norbert's journey with Mr. De began during a particularly challenging time. Father Norbert had been wrestling with a complex issue that had plagued his work for years. Technical problems with the documents Father Norbert provided had created a significant barrier, and the timely resolution of this matter was crucial. If unresolved, thousands of students would face the possibility of being unable to register for high school where he served as the principal, jeopardizing their academic futures.

Desperate for a solution, Father Norbert sought a meeting with Mr. De, hoping his vast experience and respected position might help. On the appointed day, Father Norbert arrived at Modern International Academy, feeling a mix of anxiety and hope. The school's atmosphere was inviting, a testament to Mr. De's leadership. Students moved about with purpose, teachers engaged with enthusiasm, and the aura of learning was palpable.

When Father Norbert entered Mr. De's office, Father Norbert was immediately struck by his presence. He stood up to greet Father Norbert, extending a hand with a warm smile that put him at ease. His eyes, kind and attentive, conveyed a genuine interest in Father Norbert's plight.

"Please, have a seat Father Norbert," he said, motioning to the chair opposite his desk. "How can I assist you today?"

As Father Norbert explained the situation, Mr. De listened intently, nodding occasionally. His calm demeanor and focused attention made Father Norbert feel heard and respected. When Father Norbert finished, Mr. De leaned back in his chair, thoughtfully considering the problem.

"This is indeed a challenging situation," he began. "But let's not lose hope. I believe there is always a way forward, even in the most difficult circumstances."

With those words, he began to delve into the documents, examining them with meticulous care. He made a few phone calls, leveraging his extensive network and deep understanding of the educational system. Watching him work was a lesson in grace under pressure. Despite the urgency and complexity of the task, he remained composed and methodical, never losing his calm or kindness.

Hours passed, but Mr. De's determination did not waver. He navigated bureaucratic hurdles with elegance, his experience and wisdom shining through. By the end of the day, he had made significant progress, uncovering solutions that had eluded Father Norbert for years.

"Let's reconvene tomorrow Father," he said, smiling warmly. "I'm confident we'll resolve this matter soon."

True to his word, Mr. De continued to assist Father Norbert over the next few days. His dedication and perseverance were remarkable. Finally, the issue was resolved, ensuring that thousands of students could register for high school without delay. Father Norbert was overwhelmed with gratitude.

Thank you, Mr. De, Father Norbert said, his voice choked with emotion. Father Norbert couldn't express how much this means to him and the students.

He simply smiled and patted the shoulder Father Norbert. "It's my pleasure. Remember, our role as educators is to ensure that every student has the opportunity to succeed. That's our true mission."

From that moment on, Father Norbert maintained a close relationship with Mr. De. His graciousness extended beyond that one instance; it was a fundamental part of who he was. They met regularly, and each interaction left Father Norbert more inspired. His wisdom, kindness, and unwavering commitment to education became guiding principles in his own life.

Years later, Mr. De passed away, leaving a void in the hearts of many. His legacy, however, lived on through the countless lives he had touched. Whenever Father Norbert thinks about the education system, his image comes to the mind of Father Norbert—a beacon of grace and excellence.

In reflecting on his time with Mr. De, Father Norbert realizes that being close to a gracious person like Mr. De profoundly shapes one's perspective. His ability to navigate life's challenges with poise and compassion served as a beacon of inspiration. His life exemplified the importance of emulating gracious individuals, reminding us that kindness, generosity, and elegance in handling difficulties are qualities worth cultivating.

Mr. Nabarun De's legacy is a testament to the power of grace in transforming lives. Through his actions and spirit, he taught Father Norbert and many others that true greatness lies in lifting others with kindness and unwavering support. And for that, Father Norbert is eternally grateful.

Importance of emulating gracious people to guide you in cultivating gracefulness in your own life.

The Essence of Grace

"Grace isn't a little prayer you chant before receiving a meal. It's a way to live."

- Jackie Windspear

Gracefulness is more than mere politeness; it is a way of being that reflects inner strength, empathy, and resilience. Gracious individuals radiate warmth and sincerity in their interactions, making others feel valued and respected. Understanding the essence of grace helps us appreciate its transformative power in our lives.

Recognizing Grace in Others

"Gracefulness has been defined to be the outward expression of the inward harmony of the soul."

- William Hazlitt

Gracious people often exhibit qualities such as patience, empathy, humility, and generosity. They listen attentively, offer sincere compliments, and handle conflicts with diplomacy and tact. Recognizing these traits in others allows us to appreciate and learn from their example.

Princess Diana, known for her grace and compassion, captivated the world with her genuine warmth and ability to connect with people from all walks of life. Her charitable work and empathy towards those facing adversity left a lasting legacy of gracefulness.

Cultivating Empathy and Compassion

"Empathy is seeing with the eyes of another, listening with the ears of another, and feeling with the heart of another."

- Alfred Adler

Emulating gracious people involves cultivating empathy and compassion towards others. Put yourself in their shoes, actively listen to their concerns, and offer support and encouragement when needed. By extending kindness and understanding, you create meaningful connections and foster a culture of gracefulness.

Mother Teresa's unwavering dedication to serving the poorest of the poor exemplifies the transformative power of empathy and compassion. Her ability to see the humanity in every individual, regardless of their circumstances, inspires us to embrace gracefulness in our interactions.

Practicing Patience and Tolerance

"Patience is not the ability to wait but the ability to keep a good attitude while waiting."

- Joyce Meyer

Gracious individuals exhibit patience and tolerance even in challenging situations. Practice patience in your interactions, refrain from rushing to judgment, and strive to maintain a calm and composed demeanor, especially when faced with adversity or conflict.

Mahatma Gandhi's commitment to non-violence and peaceful resistance in the face of oppression demonstrates the strength and gracefulness of patience. His unwavering resolve to pursue justice through peaceful means continues to inspire movements for social change worldwide.

Expressing Gratitude and Generosity

"Gratitude is the inward feeling of kindness received. Thankfulness is the natural impulse to express that feeling. Thanksgiving is the following of that impulse."

- Henry Van Dyke

Emulate gracious people by expressing gratitude and generosity towards others. Take time to acknowledge the kindnesses you receive, whether through a heartfelt thank-you note, a small act of kindness in return, or paying it forward to others in need.

Oprah Winfrey's philanthropic efforts and commitment to giving back demonstrate the transformative power of generosity. Her foundation, the Oprah Winfrey Foundation, supports various causes, including education, health, and empowerment, reflecting her commitment to making a positive impact on the world.

Handling Criticism with Dignity

"True dignity is never gained by place, and never lost when honors are withdrawn."

- Philip Massinger

Gracious individuals handle criticism with dignity and grace, refraining from reacting defensively or taking offense. Instead, they listen attentively, consider the feedback constructively, and respond with humility and maturity, recognizing that growth often comes from challenges and feedback.

Michelle Obama, former First Lady of the United States, faced criticism and scrutiny during her time in the public eye. Her dignified response to criticism, coupled with her unwavering commitment to her values and causes, earned her widespread admiration and respect.

Navigating Conflicts with Diplomacy

"Diplomacy is the art of letting someone else have your way."

- Daniele Vare

Emulate gracious people by navigating conflicts with diplomacy and tact. Rather than resorting to confrontation or aggression, seek to understand the perspectives of others, find common ground, and work towards mutually beneficial solutions through respectful dialogue and compromise.

Nelson Mandela's leadership during South Africa's transition from apartheid to democracy exemplifies the power of diplomacy and reconciliation. His ability to forge unity among diverse communities and negotiate peaceful resolutions to conflicts earned him global acclaim as a statesman of grace and wisdom.

Leading by Example

"The best way to teach morality is to make it a habit with children."

- Aristotle

Embracing gracefulness involves leading by example and inspiring others to cultivate similar qualities in their own lives. Demonstrate kindness, integrity, and resilience in your actions, and encourage those around you to embrace gracefulness as a guiding principle in their interactions and relationships.

Fred Rogers, beloved host of the children's television show "Mister Rogers' Neighborhood," embodied gracefulness in his gentle demeanor and compassionate approach to teaching moral values. His timeless messages of kindness and empathy continue to resonate with audiences of all ages.

Conclusion: Living with Grace and Integrity

Emulating gracious people enriches our lives and elevates our interactions with others. By recognizing and cultivating qualities such as empathy, patience, gratitude, generosity, dignity, diplomacy, and leadership, we embody gracefulness in our actions and relationships.

In doing so, we create a ripple effect of positivity and kindness that reverberates throughout our communities and beyond. Embrace the opportunity to learn from the gracefulness of others, and let their example inspire you to live with greater compassion, resilience, and integrity.

Chapter- 10

Elevating Aspirational People

Encountering aspirational individuals is akin to stumbling upon a wellspring of motivation and determination. Their ambition and drive propel them forward, inspiring those around them to aim higher and strive for greatness.

In the picturesque region of Sadar Hills, Manipur, nestled in the modest village of Char Hajar, lived Sunil, a humble school peon with an unyielding spirit. Born into a poor Nepali family, Sunil had known hardship all his life. With four children to support and a wife who ran a small coffee stall, their daily existence was a constant struggle. Yet, despite the ethnic clashes and divisive violence that plagued their region, Sunil nurtured a dream—to become self-sufficient and respected in society.

Sunil's days were long and arduous. Each morning, he would rise before dawn to help his wife prepare the coffee stall before heading to St. Vincent's Public school where he worked. The children would be up soon after, and Sunil took great pride in ensuring they attended school regularly. Education, he believed, was the key to a better future.

Life in Char Hajar was fraught with challenges, particularly during the height of the insurgency. The violent conflicts often disrupted their daily lives, making it difficult for Sunil and his community to prosper. Many dreams were shattered in the turmoil, but Sunil refused to let his aspirations be one of them.

As he swept the school corridors and tended to the grounds, Sunil found solace in his work. It was during these quiet moments that he allowed himself to dream of a different life—a life where he could provide better opportunities for his children, a life where he could hold his head high in society.

One day, as Sunil was cleaning the school yard, Father Norbert who was the Vice Principal of the School approached him. Over the years, Father Norbert had come to admire Sunil's dedication and integrity. He often noticed the spark of ambition in Sunil's eyes, despite the heavy burdens he carried.

"Sunil," Father Norbert began, "I've always been impressed by your hard work and resilience. I know times are tough, but I want you to know that your efforts do not go unnoticed."

Sunil smiled humbly, grateful for the acknowledgment. "Thank you, sir. I just try to do my best for my family and this school."

Father Norbert placed a reassuring hand on Sunil's shoulder. "I believe you have the potential to achieve much more. Have you ever considered working abroad? I've heard there are opportunities in the Gulf countries that could help you improve your circumstances."

The idea ignited a spark within Sunil as many from his neighbourhood were already in the Gulf contries and had descent earning and life style back home. So he had heard stories of people finding better opportunities abroad, but it had always seemed out of reach. Now, with the Vice Principal's encouragement, the possibility felt more tangible.

"Thank you, sir," Sunil said earnestly. "I will look into it. Your words mean a lot to me."

With the moral support of his Vice Principal and guidance over and again, Sunil began to explore the possibility of working abroad. It was a daunting process, filled with bureaucratic hurdles and financial constraints, but Sunil was determined. He attended language classes, saved every extra rupee he could, and applied for various job opportunities in the Gulf countries.

Months passed, and the strain of the application process took its toll. Yet, Sunil's resolve never wavered. He continued to work diligently at the school, his dream ever-present in his mind. The Vice Principal of his school where he worked continued to offer his support, providing references and assisting with paperwork whenever possible.

Finally, after a long and arduous journey, Sunil received an offer to work as a maintenance supervisor in a prestigious hotel in Dubai. The opportunity was a dream come true, promising a better salary and the chance to uplift his family from poverty.

The day Sunil left for Dubai was bittersweet. He bid farewell to his family and the village that had been his home. His wife, though sad to see him go, was filled with pride and hope for their future.

In Dubai, Sunil's hard work and dedication quickly earned him the respect of his colleagues and superiors. He sent money home regularly, ensuring his children could continue their education and his wife could expand her coffee stall into a small café. The transformation in their lives was profound, lifting them from the shadows of poverty and giving them a new sense of dignity and hope.

Years later, Sunil returned to Char Hajar, not as a humble peon, but as a successful and respected member of his community. His journey had been long and fraught with challenges, but his unwavering ambition and the moral support of the author had propelled him to achieve his dreams.

Sunil's story became a beacon of hope in Char Hajar, inspiring others to dream big and strive for greatness, no matter their circumstances. It illustrated the importance of elevating aspirational people, of providing them with the encouragement and support needed to turn their dreams into reality.

And so, the village of Char Hajar learned that encountering aspirational individuals was akin to stumbling upon a wellspring of motivation and determination. Their ambition and drive not only propelled them forward but also inspired those around them to aim higher and strive for greatness, weaving together the essence of human connection in a tapestry of dreams and achievements.

Embracing Ambition and Drive

"Chase the vision, not the money. The money will end up following you."

- Tony Hsieh

Aspirational people are fueled by a burning desire to achieve their goals and make a positive impact. Their ambition drives them to push boundaries, overcome obstacles, and pursue excellence in their endeavors. Embracing their ambition and drive sets the stage for collaboration, growth, and innovation.

Recognizing Potential and Passion

"The future belongs to those who believe in the beauty of their dreams."

- Eleanor Roosevelt

Elevating aspirational people begins with recognizing their potential and passion. Take time to listen to their aspirations, offer encouragement, and provide support and resources to help them turn their dreams into reality. By affirming their vision and commitment, you empower them to reach new heights.

Elon Musk's visionary pursuits, from electric vehicles to space exploration, exemplify the power of ambition and passion. Despite facing numerous setbacks and skeptics, his unwavering belief in his goals has propelled him to revolutionize multiple industries.

Offering Mentorship and Guidance

"A mentor is someone who sees more talent and ability within you than you see in yourself and helps bring it out of you."

- Bob Proctor

Mentorship plays a crucial role in elevating aspirational people, providing guidance, wisdom, and support along their journey. Offer your expertise, share your experiences, and serve as a sounding board for their ideas and aspirations. Your mentorship can make a profound difference in their development and success.

Oprah Winfrey, media mogul and philanthropist, credits her success in part to the mentorship she received throughout her career. From influential teachers to seasoned professionals, their guidance and support helped shape her into the iconic figure she is today.

Celebrating Milestones and Achievements

"Success is not the key to happiness. Happiness is the key to success. If you love what you are doing, you will be successful."

- Albert Schweitzer

Elevating aspirational people involves celebrating their milestones and achievements, no matter how small. Recognize their progress, offer praise and encouragement, and celebrate their successes as if they were your own. Your support and affirmation fuel their motivation and determination to keep striving for greatness.

Serena Williams, one of the greatest tennis players of all time, credits her family for their unwavering support and celebration of her achievements. Their encouragement and pride in her accomplishments have been instrumental in her success on and off the court.

Providing Opportunities for Growth

"The only limit to our realization of tomorrow will be our doubts of today."

- Franklin D. Roosevelt

Create opportunities for aspirational people to grow and develop their skills and talents. Offer challenging projects, facilitate networking opportunities, and provide access to training and education. By investing in their growth and development, you empower them to reach their full potential.

Google's "20% time" policy, which allows employees to spend a portion of their workweek on projects of their choosing, has led to numerous innovations and breakthroughs. This culture of autonomy and experimentation encourages employees to pursue their passions and aspirations.

Building a Supportive Community

"Alone we can do so little; together we can do so much."

- Helen Keller

Elevating aspirational people involves fostering a supportive community where they can connect, collaborate, and share ideas. Create networking events, online forums, or mentorship programs to facilitate meaningful connections and collaboration. A strong community provides a valuable support system and inspires collective growth and success.

The TED Talks platform provides a global stage for aspirational individuals to share their ideas and inspire others. By amplifying their voices and connecting them with a diverse audience, TED empowers speakers to catalyze positive change and innovation worldwide.

Encouraging Resilience and Perseverance

"The only way to do great work is to love what you do. If you haven't found it yet, keep looking. Don't settle."

- Steve Jobs

Elevating aspirational people requires encouraging resilience and perseverance in the face of challenges and setbacks. Emphasize the importance of resilience, share stories of perseverance, and offer support and encouragement during difficult times. Your belief in their potential helps them stay focused and motivated on their journey.

J.K. Rowling, author of the Harry Potter series, faced numerous rejections before finding success. Her resilience and determination to pursue her passion for writing eventually led to one of the bestselling book series of all time, inspiring millions of readers around the world.

Fostering Innovation and Creativity

"Innovation distinguishes between a leader and a follower."

- Steve Jobs

Elevating aspirational people involves fostering an environment that encourages innovation and creativity. Embrace diversity of thought, challenge conventional wisdom, and create space for experimentation and exploration. By nurturing a culture of innovation, you inspire aspirational individuals to think boldly and push the boundaries of what is possible.

Airbnb, founded by Brian Chesky, Joe Gebbia, and Nathan Blecharczyk, revolutionized the hospitality industry through innovative thinking and disruptive technology. Their aspiration to create a global community of hosts and travelers has transformed the way people travel and connect worldwide.

Conclusion: Empowering Dreams and Ambitions

Elevating aspirational people is not just about supporting individual aspirations; it's about empowering dreams and ambitions that have the potential to change the world. By recognizing potential and passion, offering mentorship and guidance, celebrating milestones and achievements, providing opportunities for growth, building a supportive community, encouraging resilience and perseverance, and fostering innovation and creativity, we create a fertile ground for dreams to flourish and ambitions to soar.

In doing so, we contribute to a culture of empowerment and possibility, where every individual has the opportunity to realize their full potential and make a meaningful impact on the world. Embrace the opportunity to elevate aspirational people in your life, and let their dreams inspire you to reach new heights of greatness.

Chapter- 11

Supporting Strength

Encountering strong individuals is akin to encountering pillars of resilience and fortitude. Their inner strength and determination inspire admiration and reverence.

In the serene town of Derapather, De Paul Boys Home stood as a sanctuary of learning and growth for many young men. The boarding school, nestled amidst lush greenery and the gentle hum of nature, was more than just a place of education; it was a community where bonds were forged and values instilled.

One stormy night, the tranquility of Derapather was shattered. Fierce winds and torrential rain wreaked havoc, leaving destruction in their wake. Among the hardest hit was Mrs. Clara, an elderly widow who lived alone at the edge of town. The storm had reduced her modest home to rubble, and though advanced in age, her spirit remained unbroken. Determined to rebuild, she set about the daunting task, but her frailty and lack of resources soon made it clear that she couldn't do it alone.

Word of Mrs. Clara's plight spread quickly through the town and reached the ears of the students at De Paul Boys Home. Known for their camaraderie and sense of community, the boys felt a deep empathy for the widow. They decided to act, inspired by her resilience and fortitude.

One evening, a group of boys gathered in their common room, discussing how they could help. "Mrs. Clara is trying to build her house all by herself," said Milan, one of the senior students. "She's been through so much, and yet she refuses to give up. We can't let her face this alone."

The boys nodded in agreement. Their admiration for Mrs. Clara's strength was palpable, and they were determined to support her in any way they could.

The next morning, they visited Mrs. Clara. She was in her yard, attempting to lift a heavy beam with trembling hands. Seeing the boys, her eyes filled with a mixture of surprise and relief.

"Jisuna Rasong Ambi which means in Garo language Greetings grand mother," said Milan, stepping forward. "We heard about your situation, and we're here to help. You don't have to do this alone."

Tears welled in Mrs. Clara's eyes as she thanked the boys. "You boys are a blessing. I've been trying so hard, but it's been difficult. Thank you, thank you so much."

With renewed energy and a sense of purpose, the boys set to work. They divided tasks among themselves, some clearing debris, others bringing in materials, and a few working on the structure itself. Their teamwork was seamless, and their spirits high, driven by the desire to ease Mrs. Clara's burden.

In addition to the physical labor, the boys made sure Mrs. Clara was well taken care of. They brought her meals from the school cafeteria, ensuring she was nourished and rested. Each meal was an opportunity for her to share stories of her past, her late husband, and the life she once had. These moments of connection deepened the bond between Mrs. Clara and the boys, turning what was initially an act of charity into a genuine relationship.

As the days passed, the new house began to take shape. The boys marveled at Mrs. Clara's determination. Despite her frailty, she insisted on contributing wherever she could, her spirit unyielding.

One evening, after a long day of work, the boys sat with Mrs. Clara around a small fire. The house was nearly complete, and the sense of accomplishment was tangible.

"You've all shown such incredible strength," said Mrs. Clara, her voice filled with gratitude. "Not just in building this house, but in your compassion and kindness. You've reminded me that even the strongest among us need support sometimes."

Milan and Simon his companion smiled and replied, "We've learned so much from you, Mrs. Clara. Your determination has inspired us. Strength isn't just about physical ability; it's about the spirit, the will to keep going despite the odds."

As the house was finally completed, the boys gathered for a small celebration. The entire town came together to honor Mrs. Clara's resilience and the boys' unwavering support. It was a testament to the power of community, where strength was not just an individual trait but a collective force.

Through their efforts, the boys at De Paul Boys Home learned an invaluable lesson: supporting strength means recognizing and reinforcing the fortitude within others. It's about offering help, encouragement, and compassion, enabling those who are strong in spirit to achieve their goals and dreams.

Mrs. Clara's new home stood as a symbol of resilience, community, and the profound impact of supporting strength. And in the hearts of the boys, the experience left an indelible mark, teaching them the true essence of human connection and the power of coming together in times of need.

Acknowledging Inner Strength

"Strength does not come from physical capacity. It comes from an indomitable will."

- Mahatma Gandhi

Strong individuals possess a resilience that enables them to weather life's storms with grace and determination. Their inner strength, forged through adversity and challenges, is a testament to their unwavering resolve and courage. Recognizing and acknowledging their strength is the first step in offering meaningful support.

Providing Emotional Support

"Being deeply loved by someone gives you strength, while loving someone deeply gives you courage."

- Lao Tzu

Strong people often bear burdens silently, but everyone can benefit from emotional support. Be a compassionate listener, offer words of encouragement, and provide a safe space for them to express their feelings. Your empathy and understanding can provide a source of comfort and strength during difficult times.

A friend going through a challenging period in their life may find solace in your presence and willingness to listen without judgment. Your support allows them to feel seen and heard, reinforcing their inner strength.

Offering Practical Assistance

"Helping one person might not change the whole world, but it could change the world for one person."

- Unknown

Strong individuals may face practical challenges that require assistance. Offer your help in tangible ways, whether it's running errands, providing transportation, or helping with household tasks. Your acts of kindness can alleviate their burden and demonstrate your support in a meaningful manner.

A coworker juggling multiple responsibilities may appreciate your offer to assist with a project deadline or provide coverage during a busy period. Your willingness to pitch in demonstrates solidarity and reinforces their strength.

Celebrating Their Achievements

"Strength does not come from winning. Your struggles develop your strengths. When you go through hardships and decide not to surrender, that is strength."

- Arnold Schwarzenegger

Strong people often achieve remarkable feats despite facing significant obstacles. Celebrate their achievements, no matter how small, and acknowledge the effort and determination they have invested. Your recognition of their accomplishments validates their strength and resilience.

A family member overcoming a health challenge may reach a milestone in their recovery journey. Celebrate their progress with a heartfelt gesture or congratulatory message, affirming their strength and perseverance.

Being a Source of Encouragement

"Encourage yourself, believe in yourself, and love yourself. Never doubt who you are."

- Stephanie Lahart

Strong individuals may doubt themselves at times, but your encouragement can bolster their confidence and resolve. Offer words of affirmation, remind them of their capabilities, and inspire them to keep pushing forward. Your belief in their potential fuels their determination to overcome obstacles.

A friend pursuing a daunting goal may encounter setbacks along the way. Your words of encouragement and reassurance that they are capable of overcoming challenges can reignite their motivation and determination.

Standing by Them Through Challenges

"True strength is keeping everything together when everyone expects you to fall apart."

- Unknown

Strong individuals may face moments of vulnerability and uncertainty. Stand by them through the ups and downs, offering unwavering support and solidarity. Your steadfast presence provides them with the assurance that they are not alone in their journey.

A colleague navigating a turbulent period in their personal life may appreciate your consistent support and understanding as they navigate challenges. Your loyalty and solidarity serve as a source of strength during difficult times.

Respecting Their Boundaries

"Respect for ourselves guides our morals, respect for others guides our manners."

- Laurence Sterne

Strong individuals may value their independence and autonomy. Respect their boundaries and preferences, allowing them to navigate challenges in their own way and at their own pace. Your understanding and respect reinforce their sense of agency and self-reliance.

A family member dealing with a sensitive issue may prefer to handle it privately and may not welcome unsolicited advice or intervention. Respect their boundaries and offer support in a manner that aligns with their needs and preferences.

Expressing Gratitude for Their Strength

"Gratitude makes sense of our past, brings peace for today, and creates a vision for tomorrow."

- Melody Beattie

Strong individuals may not always realize the impact of their strength on others. Express your gratitude for their resilience and fortitude, acknowledging the inspiration and encouragement they provide. Your words of appreciation validate their efforts and reinforce their sense of purpose.

A mentor who has guided you through challenges and setbacks may not be aware of the profound influence they have had on your life. Express your gratitude for their unwavering support and guidance, affirming the significance of their strength.

Conclusion: Standing Tall Together

Supporting strong people is not just about offering assistance; it's about standing beside them as allies and champions. By acknowledging their inner strength, providing emotional support, offering practical assistance, celebrating their achievements, being a source of encouragement, standing by them through challenges, respecting their boundaries, and expressing gratitude for their strength, we affirm their resilience and fortitude.

In doing so, we strengthen our bonds of solidarity and foster a culture of compassion and support. Embrace the opportunity to uplift and empower strong individuals in your life, and let their strength inspire you to stand tall in the face of adversity.

Chapter- 12

Bless The Godly

Encountering godly individuals is akin to stumbling upon beacons of spiritual light and wisdom. Their devout faith and exemplary lives inspire reverence and admiration.

In the quaint village of Sikaripather, nestled between rolling hills and whispering forests, the presence of Father GK Vikash was a beacon of spiritual light and wisdom. This aged Catholic priest had served the village for decades in this area, his devotion to God and his community unwavering. His humble demeanor and radiant faith inspired reverence and admiration among all who knew him.

Father Vikash's days were filled with simple yet profound routines. Each morning, he would rise before dawn and walk to the small chapel at the heart of the village. The chapel, with its whitewashed walls and modest steeple, was a place of solace and spiritual refuge for the villagers. As the first rays of sunlight filtered through the stained glass windows, Father Vikash would begin his prayers, his voice a soft murmur in the stillness of the early morning.

The villagers of Sikaripather held a deep respect for Father Vikash, not only for his devout faith but also for the kindness and wisdom he imparted. He was a living testament to the virtues he preached, embodying patience, humility, and compassion in every interaction. Children and adults alike would often seek his counsel, knowing that his words were filled with divine insight and gentle guidance.

One such individual was Sabina, a young woman struggling with the recent loss of her father. Her grief was a heavy burden, and she found herself wandering to the chapel one afternoon, hoping to find solace in its serene atmosphere. She found Father Vikash tending to the garden outside, his hands deftly pruning the roses that lined the chapel's path.

"Father," she began hesitantly, "I don't know how to move on. My heart feels so heavy."

Father Vikash looked up, his eyes filled with understanding and compassion. He motioned for her to sit on a nearby bench. "Grief is a journey, Sabina," he said softly. "It is not something to move on from, but something to carry with you. In time, it will become a part of who you are, shaping you into a stronger, more compassionate person."

Sabina listened, her tears flowing freely as Father Vikash spoke of the eternal love of God and the promise of reunion in the afterlife. His words were like balm to her wounded heart, offering her a sense of peace she had not felt since her father's passing.

As the weeks passed, Sabina continued to visit Father Vikash, each encounter bringing her closer to healing. She wasn't the only one who sought his wisdom. The villagers would often gather in the chapel on Sunday mornings, their faces lit with anticipation as

Father Vikash delivered his sermons. His messages were simple yet profound, often drawn from everyday life in Sikaripather. He spoke of the importance of community, the power of forgiveness, and the endless love of God.

Father Vikash's influence extended beyond the chapel walls. He was known to visit the sick and the elderly, bringing comfort and companionship to those who were often forgotten. His presence was a reminder of God's love, a light that shone brightly even in the darkest of times.

One particularly harsh winter, the village faced an unprecedented storm that left many families without food and warmth. Father Vikash, despite his age, organized a relief effort, mobilizing the villagers to gather supplies and distribute them to those in need. His tireless efforts and unwavering faith inspired the entire village to come together, embodying the very spirit of compassion and community he had always preached.

Years passed, and Father Vikash grew older, his steps slower, his voice a bit softer. But his spirit remained as vibrant as ever. On his 90th birthday, the entire village of Sikaripather gathered to celebrate the man who had been their spiritual guide for so long. It was a joyous occasion filled with laughter, music, and heartfelt tributes.

As the sun set, casting a golden glow over the village, Father Vikash stood before his beloved community one last time. "My dear friends," he began, his voice filled with emotion, "it has been my greatest honor to serve you all these years. Remember that the love of God is always with you, guiding you, and lighting your path. Be kind to one another, and let your faith be a beacon of hope for all."

Father Vikash was diagnonsed with cancer that evening and was asked by the doctor for a surgery and retirement if recovered from his illness. He left the village that night unprepared, the people were sad to miss their beloved priest, his life a testament to the profound impact one godly individual can have on a community. His legacy lived on in the hearts of the villagers of Sikaripather, a shining example of the power of faith, compassion, and human connection. And so, the village continued to thrive, blessed by the memory of the godly man who had touched their lives in ways they would never forget.

Recognizing Spiritual Excellence

"True godliness leaves the world convinced beyond a shadow of a doubt that the only explanation for you is Jesus."

- Matt Chandler

Godly people exude a presence of peace, love, and humility that is unmistakable. Their faith is not just a belief system but a way of life, evident in their actions, words, and character. Recognizing and acknowledging their spiritual excellence is the first step in offering them blessings.

Extending Words of Encouragement

"The world can be a tough place, but the presence of godly people reminds us that there is still goodness and light in the world."

- Unknown

Offering words of encouragement to godly individuals affirms their commitment to their faith and inspires them to continue their journey with steadfastness. Express your appreciation for their spiritual example and the positive impact they have on others.

A friend known for their unwavering faith may appreciate your heartfelt words of encouragement, acknowledging the strength and inspiration they provide through their godly example.

Praying for Their Well-being

"Prayer is not asking. It is a longing of the soul. It is daily admission of one's weakness. It is better in prayer to have a heart without words than words without a heart." - Mahatma Gandhi

Praying for godly people is a powerful way to bless them. Lift them up in prayer, asking for God's guidance, protection, and blessings upon their lives and endeavors. Your prayers serve as a source of spiritual support and affirmation.

Setting aside time to pray for a spiritual leader, mentor, or friend demonstrates your genuine care and concern for their spiritual well-being and the challenges they may face in their journey of faith.

Offering Acts of Kindness

"Kindness is a language that the deaf can hear and the blind can see."

- Mark Twain

Acts of kindness are tangible expressions of blessing for godly individuals. Extend gestures of love, compassion, and support, whether through small acts of service, thoughtful gifts, or expressions of appreciation. Your kindness reflects God's love and grace in action.

Offering to assist a church volunteer or spiritual leader with tasks or responsibilities demonstrates your appreciation for their service and dedication to their faith community.

Sharing Inspirational Resources

"Words have the power to inspire, motivate, and heal. Speak wisely."

- Unknown

Sharing inspirational resources such as books, articles, podcasts, or sermons can nourish the spiritual growth and enrichment of godly individuals. Offer recommendations that align with their interests and spiritual journey, providing them with encouragement and insight.

Recommending a book or podcast that has personally impacted your spiritual journey can ignite meaningful conversations and deepen your connection with a godly friend or mentor.

Honoring Their Wisdom and Guidance

"The wise inherit honor, but fools get only shame."

- Proverbs 3:35

Godly individuals often possess wisdom and insight cultivated through their faith journey. Honor their wisdom and guidance by seeking their counsel, listening attentively to their advice, and applying their teachings to your own life. Your respect and reverence affirm their spiritual leadership and influence.

Seeking guidance from a spiritual mentor or elder in times of uncertainty or difficulty demonstrates humility and a willingness to learn from their wisdom and experience.

Demonstrating Respect and Reverence

"Respect for ourselves guides our morals, respect for others guides our manners."

- Laurence Sterne

Demonstrate respect and reverence for godly individuals in your words and actions. Show humility, listen attentively, and honor their faith journey and spiritual convictions. Your respect reinforces the significance of their spiritual leadership and example.

Attending a religious service or ceremony with a godly friend or mentor demonstrates your respect for their faith tradition and the importance of their spiritual practices in their life.

Celebrating Their Spiritual Milestones

"Let us remember that the life we lead is a testimony of God's grace and goodness."

- Unknown

Celebrate the spiritual milestones and achievements of godly individuals, whether it's baptism, confirmation, ordination, or other significant events in their faith journey. Your participation and encouragement affirm the importance of these milestones and the impact of their faith on their life.

Attending a friend's baptism or confirmation ceremony and expressing your joy and support for their decision to publicly profess their faith reinforces the significance of the occasion and the strength of their spiritual commitment.

Conclusion: Radiating Spiritual Blessings

Blessing godly people is not just about offering prayers or acts of kindness; it's about radiating spiritual blessings that affirm their faith and inspire their spiritual journey. By extending words of encouragement, praying for their well-being, offering acts of kindness, sharing inspirational resources, honoring their wisdom and guidance, demonstrating respect and reverence, and celebrating their spiritual milestones, we affirm the significance of their spiritual excellence.

In doing so, we contribute to a culture of spiritual growth, enrichment, and empowerment, where godly individuals are uplifted and encouraged to continue shining as beacons of light and love in the world. Embrace the opportunity to bless godly people in your life, and let their spiritual example inspire you to deepen your own faith journey.

Chapter- 13

Honoring Wisdom and Experience of the Aged

Encountering elderly individuals offers a unique opportunity to connect with reservoirs of wisdom and experience. Their life journey, marked by trials and triumphs, provides valuable lessons and insights that enrich our own lives.

In the rugged hills of Manipur, where mist clung to ancient trees and the echoes of insurgency reverberated, lived an aged Catholic Catechist named Basil. His big cross around his neck bore the weight of years, and his eyes held the stories of a thousand sunsets.

Mr. Basil had served the remote village for decades. As Catechist of the humble church and educator at St. Vincent's Academy, he wove faith and knowledge into the lives of children. His hands, gnarled from countless rosaries and chalk dust, carried the essence of compassion.

But the insurgents—the shadowy figures who moved through the hills like ghosts—were not blind to Mr. Basil's influence. They saw him as a beacon of hope, a bridge between faith and reason. His wisdom transcended their ideology, and his age commanded respect.

One moonless night, they came—a group of armed men, their faces masked. They surrounded the small rectory, their rifles glinting in the darkness. Mr. Basil knelt in prayer, rosary beads slipping through his fingers.

"Old man," their leader sneered, "your faith won't save you."

Mr. Basil rose, his gaze steady. "My faith," he said, "is not a shield. It's a lantern that guides."

They demanded information—names, secrets, alliances. But Mr. Basil spoke of love, forgiveness, and the shared humanity that transcended borders. His words were like rain on parched earth, softening hearts.

The insurgents hesitated. "Why do you stay?" one of them asked. "Why not flee?"

"Because," Mr. Basil replied, "these hills are my home. These children are my flock. And wisdom, my friend, is not bound by age."

The leader stepped forward, his rifle lowered. "We've lost our way," he confessed. "Our cause blurs into violence. But you—you remind us of purpose."

And so, they left. Not in defeat, but in reverence. They honored Mr. Basil-the aged priest who had weathered storms, tended wounds, and sown seeds of compassion.

As dawn painted the hills, Catechist Basil stood on the church steps. The insurgents vanished into the mist, leaving behind a single message etched on the door:

"To the Keeper of Wisdom, may your light endure."

And Mr. Basil knew that honoring the aged was not just a duty it was the fragile thread that held their fractured world together.

Embracing the Wisdom of Age

"Respect for the aged is an important social norm. They have lived long and have much experience."

- Confucius

Elderly individuals possess a wealth of knowledge and wisdom accumulated over a lifetime of experiences. Embrace the opportunity to learn from their insights, perspectives, and life lessons, recognizing the value of their wisdom in navigating life's challenges.

Listening Attentively to Their Stories

"Old age is like a plane flying through a storm. Once you're aboard, there's nothing you can do."

- Golda Meir

Listening attentively to the stories and experiences of the elderly honors their life journey and preserves their legacy for future generations. Take time to engage in meaningful conversations, asking open-ended questions and showing genuine interest in their memories and reflections.

Spending an afternoon with an elderly neighbor, listening to their recollections of past adventures and historical events, fosters a sense of connection and appreciation for their rich life experiences.

Seeking Their Guidance and Advice

"Respect the old when you are young. Help the weak when you are strong. Confess the fault when you are wrong. Because one day in life, you will be old, weak, and wrong."

- *Unknown*

Seeking guidance and advice from the elderly demonstrates humility and respect for their wisdom and experience. Consult them on matters of life, career, and relationships, recognizing the depth of insight they offer from years of living and learning.

Seeking career advice from a retired mentor who has navigated similar challenges and transitions provides valuable perspective and guidance in making informed decisions for your own professional journey.

Valuing Their Contributions to Society

"We must appreciate the elderly and learn from their experiences and wisdom."

- Lailah Gifty Akita

Elderly individuals have made significant contributions to society through their work, service, and leadership. Acknowledge and celebrate their achievements, recognizing the impact they have had on their communities and the legacy they leave behind.

Honoring a veteran's service and sacrifice on Veterans Day or expressing gratitude to a retired teacher for their dedication to education highlights the enduring impact of their contributions to society.

Providing Support and Assistance

"To care for those who once cared for us is one of the highest honors."

- Tia Walker

Offering support and assistance to the elderly demonstrates compassion and respect for their well-being and dignity. Extend a helping hand with daily tasks, transportation, or companionship, easing their burdens and showing appreciation for their presence in your life.

Assisting an elderly relative with grocery shopping or household chores allows them to maintain their independence and quality of life while fostering a sense of connection and care within the family.

Upholding Their Dignity and Autonomy

"Age is an issue of mind over matter. If you don't mind, it doesn't matter."

- Mark Twain

Respecting the elderly involves upholding their dignity and autonomy, recognizing their right to make decisions and live life on their own terms. Avoid patronizing or infantilizing language and treat them with the same courtesy and respect you would expect for yourself.

Consulting an elderly parent or grandparent on important family decisions and respecting their wishes regarding their living arrangements and medical care honors their autonomy and independence.

Celebrating Milestones and Achievements

"Age is opportunity no less than youth itself."

- Henry Wadsworth Longfellow

Celebrating milestones and achievements in the lives of the elderly acknowledges their resilience and vitality, affirming their continued significance and contributions to the world. Whether it's a milestone birthday, anniversary, or personal accomplishment, take time to honor and celebrate their life journey.

Organizing a surprise birthday party for an elderly family member or commemorating a significant anniversary with a special gathering of friends and loved ones recognizes the joy and significance of their life milestones.

Advocating for Their Rights and Well-being

"Ageism is as odious as racism and sexism."

- Claude Pepper

Advocating for the rights and well-being of the elderly promotes social justice and equality, ensuring they have access to essential resources, healthcare, and support services. Stand up against ageism and discrimination, advocating for policies and practices that uphold the dignity and rights of older adults.

Participating in advocacy efforts for affordable healthcare and social services for the elderly or supporting initiatives to combat elder abuse and neglect demonstrates a commitment to promoting the well-being and dignity of older adults in society.

Conclusion: Honoring the Legacy of Age

Respecting the elderly is not just a cultural norm; it is a reflection of our shared humanity and interconnectedness across generations. By embracing the wisdom of age, listening attentively to their stories, seeking their guidance and advice, valuing their contributions to society, providing support and assistance, upholding their dignity and autonomy, celebrating milestones and achievements, and advocating for their rights and well-being, we honor the legacy of age and affirm the enduring value of every individual's life journey.

In doing so, we foster a culture of respect, compassion, and inclusion, where the wisdom and experience of the elderly are treasured and celebrated. Embrace the opportunity to respect the elderly in your life, and let their stories and insights inspire you to live with greater wisdom, compassion, and gratitude.

Chapter- 14

Empowering The Vulnerable

Encountering individuals facing adversity or struggling with challenges presents an opportunity to extend a helping hand and offer support.

In the remote village of Hojai District of Assam, nestled amidst lush tea plantations and mist-kissed hills, lived a woman named Kamala Roy. Kamala was no stranger to adversity. Her husband had passed away, leaving her with three young children and a crumbling mud-brick house.

The monsoons were relentless, flooding the village paths and seeping into homes. Kamala's neighbors-Rina and Suresh were in similar situations. Rina's husband was a daily wage laborer, and Suresh, a retired school teacher, struggled to make ends meet.

One evening, as the rain drummed on Kamala's roof, she gathered her neighbors. "We can't change the weather," she said, "but we can strengthen each other."

And so, they formed the Village Resilience Circle. Their mission? To empower the vulnerable—to weave safety nets of compassion and practical support.

1. The Seed of Education :

Kamala opened her home for evening classes. Rina taught basic literacy, while Suresh shared stories of historical figures who rose from poverty.

The children sat on bamboo mats, their eyes wide. Kamala whispered, "Education is the seed that grows into resilience."

2. The Thread of Empathy :

When Rina fell ill, Kamala cooked meals for her family. Suresh repaired her leaky roof.

"Empathy," Kamala said, "is the thread that binds us."

3. The Shelter of Collective Strength :

They built a community center—a sturdy brick building that doubled as a school during the day and a refuge during storms. - Kamala painted a lotus on the entrance a reminder that even in mud, beauty blooms.

4. The Harvest of Hard Work :

Kamala's children helped in the tea gardens. Rina's husband planted vegetables. Suresh taught math to eager minds.

"Hard work," Kamala declared, "is the harvest we share."

5. The Lotus Blooms :

One day, a government official visited. He marveled at the community center, the children reading under the lotus mural.

"How did you do it?" he asked.

Kamala smiled. "We empowered the vulnerable. We wove lives together."

Years passed. The Village Resilience Circle expanded. Kamala's children became doctors, Rina's daughter a teacher, and Suresh's grandson an engineer.

On Kamala's 70th birthday, they gathered under the lotus mural. The rain had stopped, and the sun painted the hills gold. Kamala raised her cup of chai. "To resilience," she said.

And the village echoed, "To resilience!"

The lotus bloomed, its petals unfurling-a testament to Kamala's vision. Empowering the vulnerable wasn't charity; it was the art of weaving lives.

Embracing Empathy and Compassion

"Empathy is seeing with the eyes of another, listening with the ears of another, and feeling with the heart of another."

- Alfred Adler

Empathy and compassion are foundational to strengthening the weak. Take time to understand their struggles, listen to their concerns, and offer support without judgment. Your empathy creates a safe space for vulnerability and fosters a sense of connection and understanding.

Providing Practical Assistance

"Helping one person might not change the whole world, but it could change the world for one person."

- Unknown

Offering practical assistance to those in need strengthens their resilience and resourcefulness. Extend a helping hand with tasks or responsibilities, provide access to essential resources or services, and offer guidance in navigating challenges. Your support empowers them to take positive steps towards overcoming obstacles.

Volunteering at a local food bank or homeless shelter provides tangible assistance to individuals experiencing food insecurity or homelessness, helping to address immediate needs and strengthen their resilience.

Offering Encouragement and Motivation

"Encourage yourself, believe in yourself, and love yourself. Never doubt who you are."

- Stephanie Lahart

Encouragement and motivation are powerful tools for strengthening the weak. Offer words of affirmation, remind them of their strengths and potential, and inspire them to persevere in the face of adversity. Your encouragement instills hope and confidence, fueling their determination to overcome obstacles.

Providing encouragement to a friend or family member pursuing a challenging goal or facing setbacks in their personal or professional life boosts their morale and reinforces their belief in their ability to succeed.

Cultivating Resilience and Self-Efficacy

"The human capacity for burden is like bamboo – far more flexible than you'd ever believe at first glance."

- Jodi Picoult

Empowering vulnerable individuals involves cultivating resilience and self-efficacy. Help them recognize their inner strength and capacity to overcome adversity, and encourage them to develop coping strategies and problem-solving skills. Your support equips them with the tools they need to navigate challenges with confidence and determination.

Offering resilience-building workshops or support groups for individuals experiencing trauma or adversity provides a supportive environment for learning and growth, empowering them to cultivate resilience and navigate challenges effectively.

Fostering a Supportive Community

"Alone we can do so little; together we can do so much."

- Helen Keller

Creating a supportive community strengthens vulnerable individuals by providing a network of encouragement, guidance, and solidarity. Foster connections with peers, mentors, and support groups, and encourage collaboration and mutual support. A strong community provides a source of comfort, empowerment, and resilience.

Establishing a peer support group for individuals recovering from addiction or mental health challenges creates a safe and supportive space for sharing experiences, providing encouragement, and fostering mutual growth and healing.

Advocating for Systemic Change

"Injustice anywhere is a threat to justice everywhere."

- Martin Luther King Jr.

Empowering vulnerable individuals involves advocating for systemic change to address underlying barriers and inequalities. Speak out against injustice and discrimination, advocate for policies and practices that promote equity and inclusion, and support organizations working to create positive social change. Your advocacy amplifies their voices and promotes systemic solutions to empower vulnerable populations.

Participating in advocacy efforts for affordable housing, healthcare access, or education equity addresses systemic barriers that perpetuate poverty and vulnerability, empowering individuals and communities to thrive.

Promoting Mental Health and Well-being

"Self-care is giving the world the best of you, instead of what's left of you."

- Katie Reed

Supporting vulnerable individuals includes promoting mental health and well-being. Encourage self-care practices, such as mindfulness, relaxation techniques, and seeking professional support when needed. Create spaces for open dialogue about mental health and reduce stigma surrounding seeking help. Your support promotes resilience and fosters a culture of well-being.

Organizing mental health awareness events or workshops in schools, workplaces, or communities promotes understanding and support for individuals struggling with mental health challenges, strengthening their resilience and fostering a culture of compassion and empathy.

Conclusion: Empowering Vulnerability, Embracing Strength

Strengthening the weak is not just about providing temporary assistance; it's about empowering vulnerability and fostering resilience and self-efficacy. By embracing empathy and compassion, offering practical assistance, providing encouragement and motivation, cultivating resilience and self-efficacy, fostering a supportive community, advocating for systemic change, promoting mental health and well-being, we empower vulnerable individuals to overcome obstacles and thrive.

In doing so, we create a more inclusive and equitable society where every individual has the opportunity to reach their full potential and contribute to the collective well-being. Embrace the opportunity to strengthen the weak in your life, and let your support and compassion inspire them to embrace their inner strength and resilience.

Chapter- 15

Nurturing Determination and Resilience

Encountering hardworking individuals offers a glimpse into the power of dedication and perseverance. Their relentless pursuit of excellence inspires admiration and respect.

In the heart of Karbi Anglong district, Assam, where emerald hills rolled like ancient tales and the air carried whispers of resilience, stood the remote village of Klurdung Gaon. Here, life unfolded at its own pace-a rhythm set by monsoons and harvests.

Meet Rina Engti, a woman of quiet strength. She had returned to her ancestral village after years of education and work in the bustling city. As the newly appointed principal of the village school, she carried dreams like seeds in her pocket.

The school was a modest building—a single room with bamboo walls and a thatched roof. The children, their eyes wide with curiosity, sat on woven mats. Rina's heart swelled as she looked at their eager faces. These were the children of farmers, weavers, and laborers—their futures woven into the fabric of the land.

The first day of school was magical. Rina taught them the alphabet, their fingers tracing invisible letters in the air. She shared stories of distant lands, of astronauts and tigers, of courage and kindness. The children listened, their eyes reflecting starlit skies.

But challenges loomed. The village had no electricity, and the nearest road was a day's trek away. Rina remembered her own journey a three hour hike through dense forests and winding trails. Yet, she believed in the Resilient Lotus the flower that bloomed even in adversity.

One evening, as the sun dipped behind the hills, Rina sat with the elders the village council under the ancient banyan tree. She shared her vision: solar panels for the school, books for the library, and hope for every child.

The elders listened, their faces etched with wisdom. Bor Sing Rongpi, the village head, spoke. "Our ancestors taught us to weather storms," he said. "Now, it's our turn to nurture resilience."

And so, they rallied. The men carried solar panels on their shoulders, trekking through rain and mud. The women wove mats for the classroom floor. The children planted saplings around the school, their small hands touching the earth with promise.

The day the solar bulbs lit up, the village rejoiced. Children danced, their laughter echoing through the hills. Rina watched, tears in her eyes. The Resilient Lotus had bloomed the school was now a beacon of light.

Rina taught more than academics. She taught courage to Bule Thang Kuki, the shy girl who loved to draw, and to Amri Rongpi, the boy who dreamed of becoming a doctor. She taught kindness to Biren Teron, who shared his lunch with a hungry friend, and to Chondro Sing Teron, who helped mend broken slates.

Years passed. The school expanded a second room, a playground, and a garden where marigolds greeted the sun. Rina's heart swelled with pride. The children-her lotus blooms-blossomed into doctors, teachers, and artists.

On her last day as principal, Rina stood under the banyan tree. The elders gathered, their eyes filled with gratitude. Numal Momin, the local MLA, spoke. "You've nurtured determination," he said. "These children will rise unbreakable." As Rina left, she carried memories the laughter, the handwritten notes, and the Resilient Lotus that would forever bloom in her heart.

Applying resilience to your work or community projects involves cultivating a mindset and adopting practical strategies. Here are some steps you can take:

1. **Mindset Shift :**

   o Understand that setbacks are part of any journey. Resilience isn't about avoiding challenges; it's about bouncing back stronger. - Embrace a growth mindset—see failures as opportunities for learning and growth.

2. **Set Clear Goals :**

   o Define your objectives clearly. Break them down into smaller, achievable steps. - When faced with obstacles, revisit your goals to stay focused.

3. **Build a Support Network :**

   o Surround yourself with positive, like-minded individuals. Seek mentors, peers, or community members who inspire you. - Collaborate with others on community projects. Collective resilience is powerful.

4. **Adaptability :**

   o Be flexible. Plans may change, unexpected events may occur. Adaptability allows you to pivot without losing momentum. - Learn from nature—the bamboo bends in the storm but doesn't break.

5. **Self-Care :**

   o Resilience starts within. Prioritize physical health, mental well-being, and emotional balance.

   o Practice mindfulness, meditation, or hobbies that recharge you.

6. **Learn from Setbacks:**

   o Analyze failures objectively. What went wrong? What can you improve?

   o Use setbacks as stepping stones. Edison didn't fail; he found 10,000 ways that didn't work.

7. **Celebrate Small Wins :**

   o Acknowledge progress, even if it's incremental. Celebrate achievements along the way.

   o Small victories build resilience and motivation.

8. **Stay Solution-Focused :**

   o Instead of dwelling on problems, focus on solutions. Break down challenges into actionable steps.

   o Seek creative alternatives when faced with roadblocks.

9. **Storytelling :**

    o Share stories of resilience within your community. Highlight individuals who overcame adversity.

    o Stories inspire and create a sense of collective strength.

10. **Learn from Nature :**

    o Look at the lotus, the banyan tree, or the bamboo. They thrive despite harsh conditions.

    o Draw inspiration from their resilience. Remember, resilience isn't a fixed trait-it's a skill you can develop. Apply these principles to your work, projects, and interactions within your community.

Recognizing Dedication and Effort

"The only limit to our realization of tomorrow will be our doubts of today." - Franklin D. Roosevelt

Hardworking individuals demonstrate a commitment to excellence and a willingness to invest time and effort in pursuing their goals. Recognize and acknowledge their dedication and effort, affirming the value of their contributions and the impact of their hard work.

Offering Words of Affirmation

"Believe you can, and you're halfway there."

- Theodore Roosevelt

Words of affirmation are a powerful source of encouragement for hardworking individuals. Offer praise and recognition for their achievements, affirming their dedication and perseverance. Your words of encouragement boost their morale and reinforce their belief in their abilities.

Praising a colleague for their diligent work ethic and outstanding performance on a project reaffirms their value to the team and motivates them to continue striving for excellence.

Providing Support and Resources

"Alone we can do so little; together we can do so much."

- Helen Keller

Offering support and resources to hardworking individuals empowers them to achieve their goals more effectively. Provide assistance with tasks or projects, offer access to training or mentorship opportunities, and create a supportive environment that fosters growth and development.

Providing access to professional development opportunities, such as workshops or seminars, equips hardworking employees with the skills and knowledge they need to advance in their careers and achieve their aspirations.

Celebrating Milestones and Achievements

"Success is not the key to happiness. Happiness is the key to success. If you love what you are doing, you will be successful."

- Albert Schweitzer

Celebrating milestones and achievements is a way to honor the hard work and dedication of individuals. Whether it's reaching a sales target, completing a project, or achieving a personal goal, take time to acknowledge and celebrate their accomplishments.

Organizing a team celebration or recognition ceremony for surpassing performance targets or completing a challenging project demonstrates appreciation for their hard work and fosters a sense of camaraderie and achievement.

Offering Constructive Feedback

"Feedback is the breakfast of champions."

- Ken Blanchard

Providing constructive feedback is essential for supporting the growth and development of hardworking individuals. Offer specific and actionable feedback that helps them identify areas for improvement and build upon their strengths. Your guidance and support contribute to their continuous learning and improvement.

Offering feedback on a colleague's presentation or project performance highlights areas of excellence and opportunities for refinement, empowering them to elevate their skills and performance.

Cultivating a Positive Work Environment

"Surround yourself with only people who are going to lift you higher."

- Oprah Winfrey

Creating a positive work environment fosters motivation and engagement among hardworking individuals. Cultivate a culture of collaboration, appreciation, and positivity that energizes and inspires them to excel. Your leadership sets the tone for a supportive and empowering workplace.

Establishing a recognition program or peer-to-peer appreciation initiative encourages employees to celebrate each other's contributions and reinforces a culture of gratitude and recognition for hard work.

Embracing a Growth Mindset

"The only way to do great work is to love what you do. If you haven't found it yet, keep looking. Don't settle."

- Steve Jobs

Encouraging a growth mindset promotes resilience and innovation among hardworking individuals. Emphasize the value of learning from failures, embracing challenges, and continuously seeking opportunities for growth and development.

Encouraging employees to pursue stretch assignments or take on new challenges empowers them to expand their skills and capabilities, fostering a culture of growth and innovation within the organization.

Conclusion: Nurturing Determination and Resilience

Encouraging the hardworking is not just about offering praise or recognition; it's about nurturing determination and resilience that propel individuals to achieve their fullest potential. By recognizing dedication and effort, offering words of affirmation, providing support and resources, celebrating milestones and achievements, offering constructive feedback, cultivating a positive work environment, embracing a growth mindset, we empower hardworking individuals to overcome obstacles and thrive.

In doing so, we foster a culture of excellence and achievement where every individual feels valued, supported, and inspired to pursue their goals with passion and purpose. Embrace the opportunity to encourage the hardworking in your life, and let your support and encouragement ignite their drive and determination to reach new heights of success.

Chapter- 16

Esteeming Kind People: Honoring Acts of Compassion and Generosity

Kindness is a profound virtue that transcends cultures and connects humanity on a fundamental level. Encountering kind individuals who consistently demonstrate compassion and generosity enriches our lives and communities.

The Taxi Driver's Gift: A Journey of Compassion

As the Howrah-Chennai mail pulled into the higly busy Howrah Station, Muna Babu was eager to reach his destination Tollyguange. The station, a hive of activity, showcased a kaleidoscope of life and movement. Muna Babu quickly secured a prepaid taxi to Tollyguange and soon found himself on a journey that would become more meaningful than he could have anticipated.

His taxi driver was an elderly man named Ashish from a remote village in Bihar. His worn hands and kind eyes spoke of countless stories of resilience and humility. As we navigated the streets, he suddenly asked if Muna Babu could wait for a few minutes. Curious, he agreed to the request of Ashish, watching as he pulled over near the Park Street area.

Ashish got out, opened the trunk, and retrieved a few packets. To Muna Babu's surprise, Ashish handed them to a destitute woman sitting on the footpath with her three children. The gratitude in her eyes was profound, and the children eagerly accepted the food, their faces lighting up with joy.

As they resumed their journey, Muna Babu couldn't contain his curiosity. "Who is that woman?" he asked.

Ashish sighed deeply before responding, "She is a homeless mother of three. They have no food or shelter. One night, as I was returning home late, I saw her begging, but no one stopped to help. I was moved by their plight and decided I couldn't ignore them. Since then, I have made it a point to bring them food whenever I can."

He continued, "I may be poor myself, living in my taxi and using public restrooms, but I cannot let this woman and her children starve. I might not be able to provide shelter, but at least I can ensure they have something to eat. Today, I was late, but I still managed to bring them some food. As long as I am in Kolkata, I want to bring a bit of joy to this family."

His words resonated deeply within Muna Babu. Here was a man who, despite his own hardships, chose to give whatever little he had to those in greater need. His selfless acts of compassion and generosity exemplified the true essence of humanity.

The encounter taught Muna Babu a profound life lesson: Kindness is not measured by the size of our wealth but by the depth of our hearts. The taxi driver's consistent compassion and generosity were not acts of convenience but of commitment. He showed Muna Babu that even in the face of personal adversity, we have the power to make a positive difference in someone else's life.

Honoring such acts of kindness is essential. They remind us of our shared humanity and the impact one individual can have on the lives of others. The taxi driver's unwavering dedication to helping a homeless family, despite his own struggles, is a testament to the boundless nature of compassion. It inspires us to look beyond our own circumstances and to reach out to those in need, knowing that even the smallest act of kindness can create ripples of hope and joy.

As Muna Babu reached his destination, he left the taxi not just with a sense of having arrived at a physical location, but with a renewed sense of purpose. The driver's story lingered with him, a powerful reminder that true wealth is found in the generosity of spirit and the kindness we extend to others.

Recognizing Acts of Kindness

"Kindness is the language which the deaf can hear and the blind can see."

- Mark Twain

Recognizing and acknowledging acts of kindness highlights the significance of these compassionate gestures. Whether it's a small act of courtesy or a grand gesture of generosity, take time to appreciate and commend the efforts of kind individuals.

Thanking a coworker who consistently brings a positive attitude and helps others in the office creates an environment where kindness is recognized and valued.

Celebrating Compassionate Individuals

"To the world, you may be one person, but to one person, you may be the world."

- Dr. Seuss

Celebrating compassionate individuals affirms their positive impact on others and encourages a culture of kindness. Organize events or initiatives that highlight and honor their contributions to fostering a more caring and supportive community.

Hosting an annual awards ceremony to recognize volunteers who have made significant contributions to community service emphasizes the value of their kindness and inspires others to follow their example.

Offering Words of Appreciation

"A warm smile is the universal language of kindness."

- William Arthur Ward

Expressing appreciation for kind individuals reinforces their positive behavior and encourages them to continue spreading kindness. Offer genuine compliments and heartfelt thanks for their acts of compassion and generosity.

Writing a thank-you note to a teacher who goes above and beyond to support their students acknowledges their kindness and dedication, reinforcing the impact of their efforts.

Providing Support and Encouragement

"Wherever there is a human being, there is an opportunity for a kindness."

- Seneca

Supporting and encouraging kind individuals ensures they feel valued and appreciated. Offer assistance with their endeavors, provide resources to amplify their efforts, and encourage them to continue making a difference.

Supporting a friend who organizes charity events by volunteering your time or helping with fundraising efforts demonstrates appreciation for their kindness and strengthens their impact.

Sharing Their Stories

"Kindness is a passport that opens doors and fashions friends. It softens hearts and molds relationships that can last lifetimes."

- Joseph B. Wirthlin

Sharing stories of kind individuals and their acts of compassion inspires others to embrace kindness in their own lives. Highlight their efforts in community newsletters, social media, or local news outlets to spread their positive influence.

Featuring a local hero who regularly volunteers at a homeless shelter in a community newsletter brings attention to their kindness and encourages others to get involved.

Creating Opportunities for Kindness

"No act of kindness, no matter how small, is ever wasted."

- Aesop

Creating opportunities for kindness within your community or organization fosters a culture of compassion and generosity. Encourage initiatives and programs that promote acts of kindness and provide platforms for kind individuals to share their talents and passions.

Establishing a "Kindness Week" in a school or workplace where everyone is encouraged to perform and share acts of kindness promotes a collective spirit of compassion and mutual support.

Encouraging a Ripple Effect

"One small act of kindness can make a big difference in someone's life."

- Roy T. Bennett

Kindness has a ripple effect, inspiring others to pay it forward. Encourage kind individuals by acknowledging their influence and motivating them to continue spreading kindness. Your esteem for their actions reinforces the importance of their contributions.

Publicly recognizing an employee who regularly mentors new hires and encourages a supportive work culture reinforces the value of their kindness and inspires others to emulate their behavior.

Building a Community of Kindness

"Kindness is a gift everyone can afford to give."

- Unknown

Building a community of kindness involves creating an environment where compassionate behavior is the norm and everyone feels valued and supported. Encourage collaboration, mutual respect, and empathy in all interactions, fostering a culture where kindness thrives.

Initiating a community garden project where neighbors work together to cultivate and share produce fosters a sense of cooperation, generosity, and mutual support, creating a tangible representation of kindness in action.

Conclusion: Honoring the Heart of Humanity

Esteeming kind people is about more than just recognizing their individual acts of compassion; it's about honoring the heart of humanity and fostering a culture where kindness is celebrated and encouraged. By recognizing acts of kindness, celebrating compassionate individuals, offering words of appreciation, providing support and encouragement, sharing their stories, creating opportunities for kindness, encouraging a ripple effect, and building a community of kindness, we affirm the importance of compassion and generosity in our lives and communities.

In doing so, we create a more inclusive, supportive, and compassionate world where every act of kindness is valued and celebrated. Embrace the opportunity to esteem kind people in your life, and let their example inspire you to cultivate and spread kindness wherever you go.

Chapter- 17

Promote The Honest : Elevating Integrity and Trust

Honesty is a cornerstone of integrity and trust, essential qualities for building strong relationships and successful communities. Encountering honest individuals who consistently demonstrate transparency and truthfulness provides a foundation for reliability and respect.

In the heart of Sadar Hills, a small town Kholep nestled between rolling meadows, lived an unassuming woman named Jescinta. She was known for her honesty, a rare gem in a world where half-truths and hidden agendas often held sway.

Jescinta ran a modest bakery, its wooden sign creaking in the breeze: Jescinta's Truthful Treats. Her pastries were more than butter and flour; they carried whispers of sincerity. Customers flocked to her shop not just for the flaky croissants or cinnamon rolls but for the warmth that enveloped them.

One day, a young boy named Thangboi entered the bakery. His eyes darted nervously, and his pockets sagged with secrets. He approached Jescinta, his voice barely audible. "I stole a candy bar," he confessed. "I'm sorry."

Jescinta's eyes crinkled with kindness. She placed a chocolate chip cookie in front of him. "Thangboi," she said, "honesty is sweeter than any treat. Return the candy, and remember this moment."

Thangboi left, clutching the cookie and newfound courage. The next day, he returned, the stolen candy bar in hand. Jescinta smiled, her apron dusted with flour. "You've made the right choice," she said. "Integrity is the icing on life's cake."

Word spread about Jescinta's bakery. It wasn't just about pastries anymore; it was a sanctuary for truth-seekers. The mayor, the librarian, even the grumpy postman all found solace within its walls. They shared their confessions over cups of chamomile tea and slices of honesty pie.

And so, Sadar Hills transformed. The town meetings became forums for open dialogue. The school curriculum included lessons on integrity. The garden club planted seeds of truth, and the annual fair awarded the most candid citizen.

Jescinta's legacy extended beyond her bakery. When she passed away, her recipe book vanished, but her spirit lingered. The townspeople whispered, "Remember Jescinta's Truthful Treats." And they did through acts of kindness, transparent conversations, and unwavering trust.

Jescinta's story reminds: Promote the honest. Elevate integrity. Trust will rise like a perfectly baked loaf, nourishing the soul of your community.

The lesson that we learn from the idyllic town of Sadar Hills:

1. The Bridge of Empathy : Sadar Hills taught its residents to listen with open hearts. The mayor, inspired by Jescinta's bakery, initiated "Walk a Mile" days. Each person paired up with someone different—teachers with students, doctors with farmers. They swapped stories, walked the town's cobblestone streets, and discovered shared dreams and fears. Empathy became the bridge that connected diverse lives.

2. The River of Forgiveness : Along side NH 37 flows the anscient Imphal river-the **Forgiveness River**. When conflicts arose, people offered flowers to the River in prayer. Each flower represented a name and a whispered apology. The wind carried these confessions, weaving forgiveness into the town's fabric. The lesson? Forgiveness isn't weakness; it's the strength to heal.

3. The Starlit Conversations : On clear nights, the townspeople gathered at the hilltop observatory. They pointed telescopes at distant constellations and shared their hopes. The **Starlit Conversations** reminded them that life's vastness held both mystery and connection. They learned that vulnerability under the stars was a powerful elixir for trust.

4. The Honesty Quilt : The local quilting club stitched a masterpiece—the **Honesty Quilt**. Each patch represented a truth shared during their weekly meetings. Some patches were vibrant, others faded, but together they formed a mosaic of authenticity. The quilt hung in the community center, reminding everyone that honesty was a collective effort.

5. The Whispering Wells : Harmony Hills had three wells—the **Wells of Truth, Kindness, and Courage**. People drew water not just for hydration but for reflection. The Wells whispered advice: "Speak your heart," "Lift others," "Leap into the unknown." The townspeople learned that wisdom flowed from within, and the Wells were their silent mentors. As you journey through these lessons, dear reader, may you find echoes of

Harmony Hills in your own life—a place where honesty, empathy, forgiveness, stargazing, and inner wells converge to create a harmonious existence.

Recognizing the Value of Honesty

"Honesty is the first chapter in the book of wisdom."

- Thomas Jefferson

Honest individuals contribute to a culture of trust and reliability. Recognize and acknowledge the value of their integrity, emphasizing how their truthfulness positively impacts relationships, workplaces, and communities.

Offering Praise for Honesty

"Honesty and transparency make you vulnerable. Be honest and transparent anyway."

- Mother Teresa

Praise honest individuals for their commitment to truthfulness, even when it may be difficult or uncomfortable. Express appreciation for their transparency and the trust they build through their actions.

Providing Opportunities for Leadership

"Leadership is not about being in charge. It is about taking care of those in your charge."

- Simon Sinek

Promote honest individuals by providing them with opportunities for leadership and greater responsibility. Their integrity sets a positive example for others and builds a foundation of trust within any organization or community.

Creating a Culture of Transparency

"Integrity is doing the right thing, even when no one is watching."

- C.S. Lewis

Cultivating a culture of transparency encourages honest behavior and reinforces the importance of integrity. Implement practices and policies that promote open communication, ethical decision-making, and accountability.

Rewarding Ethical Behavior

"Integrity is choosing your thoughts and actions based on values rather than personal gain."

- Chris Karcher

Rewarding ethical behavior underscores the importance of honesty and integrity. Recognize and reward individuals who consistently demonstrate ethical conduct, reinforcing the value of their actions.

Sharing Stories of Integrity

"Truth never damages a cause that is just."

- Mahatma Gandhi

Sharing stories of integrity and honesty inspires others to embrace these values. Highlight examples of individuals who have made significant contributions through their commitment to truthfulness and ethical behavior.

Encouraging Open Dialogue

"Honesty is the best policy. If I lose mine honor, I lose myself."

- William Shakespeare

Encouraging open dialogue about the importance of honesty and integrity fosters a culture of trust and mutual respect. Create spaces for conversations about ethical dilemmas, transparency, and the value of truthfulness in personal and professional settings.

Supporting Personal and Professional Growth

"Honesty is the fastest way to prevent a mistake from turning into a failure."

- James Altucher

Supporting the personal and professional growth of honest individuals ensures they continue to thrive and contribute positively to their communities. Provide opportunities for skill development, mentorship, and career advancement.

Building Trust through Consistency

"Trust is built with consistency."

- Lincoln Chafee

Trust is built through consistent honesty and integrity. Recognize and promote individuals who demonstrate these qualities consistently, reinforcing the importance of reliability and truthfulness in all interactions.

Conclusion: Elevating Integrity and Trust

Promoting honest people is about more than just recognizing their individual contributions; it's about elevating the values of integrity and trust in all aspects of life. By recognizing the value of honesty, offering praise for honesty, providing opportunities for leadership, creating a culture of transparency, rewarding ethical behavior, sharing stories of integrity, encouraging open dialogue, supporting personal and professional growth, and building trust through consistency, we reinforce the importance of truthfulness and ethical behavior.

In doing so, we create environments where integrity and trust are valued and promoted, fostering stronger relationships and more successful communities. Embrace the opportunity to promote honest people in your life, and let their example inspire you and others to uphold the highest standards of integrity and truthfulness.

Chapter- 18

Rewarding The Virtuous : Honoring Excellence in Character

Virtuous individuals embody the highest standards of moral and ethical behavior. Their actions, driven by principles of integrity, compassion, and justice, set a powerful example for others. Recognizing and rewarding virtuous people not only affirms their positive contributions but also encourages a culture of virtue and excellence. One such exemplary figure of virtue is Mahatma Gandhi, a paragon of nonviolence and truth. His commitment to peaceful resistance and his unwavering integrity in the face of oppression inspired countless individuals to follow his lead. Gandhi's life was a testament to the power of steadfast compassion and ethical conviction, making him a timeless symbol of virtue.

The importance of rewarding virtuous individuals is explored here offering strategies, inspirational wisdom, and real-life examples to guide you in honoring their character and fostering a culture of virtue.

Recognizing Virtue in Action

"Virtue is bold, and goodness never fearful."

- William Shakespeare

Recognizing the actions of virtuous individuals highlights the significance of their moral and ethical behavior. Whether through acts of kindness, honesty, or courage, acknowledging their virtues sets a standard for others to emulate.

In the bustling hall of fame of DPS Academy, Kolkata, there was an air of anticipation. Today, the school would honour a student not for academic prowess or athletic skill, but for something far more profound: virtue.

Sumedha, a quite presence with a heart full of kindness, had become the unsung hero of DPS Academy. She was a student who stayed late to help her peers understand complex algebra problems, who shared her lunch with those who forgot theirs, and who always had an encouraging word for the disheartened.

Father Norbert as the principal called for silence, and with beaming smile, he announced Sumedha's name. As she walked up to receive her award, the applause was thunderous. Sumedha's consistent acts of kindness had woven a tapestry of positivity throughout DPS Academy her alma mater.

This moment was more than recognition; it was a powerful message to all: virtue, in its quiet strength, is the most impactful force of all.

Publicly recognizing a student like Sumedha, who goes out of their way to help classmates and promote a positive school environment demonstrates the value of virtue in action.

Offering Praise and Gratitude

"Praise is the best auxiliary to virtue."

- Cicero

Expressing praise and gratitude to virtuous individuals reinforces their positive behavior and affirms their contributions. Sincere appreciation for their actions fosters a sense of recognition and encourages them to continue their virtuous path.

In the busy trafic of NSC Bose Road, DPS Academy was beacon of learning and safety, thanks in no small part to Paul Rudra, the watchman and school gate keeper. His vigilant eyes and warm greetings were as much a part of the school as the bricks that built it.

Paul's dedication went beyond his duty; he were the guardian of every child's well-being. When little Anna lost her way on her first day, it was Paul who comforted her with kind words and guided her to class. When the dispersal time came, he ensured every child passed safely through the grate and were handed over to the parents.

Father Norbert had the pleasure to work with such honest and good hearted man and recognized the quiet heroism in his daily vigil. A special assembly was arranged to honor him. As Paul stood before the school, he recounted Paul's act of kindness, his unwavering commitment to their safety, and his role as an unsung hero.

The Children's cheers filled the air, echoing through NSC Bose Road. Paul, once just a watchman in their eyes, were now their champions. Their story of virtue would be told for generations, inspiring all within the school walls.

This is the best example of thanking a colleague who consistently demonstrates integrity and fairness in their work builds a culture of appreciation and respect for virtuous behavior.

Providing Tangible Rewards

"Virtue is its own reward."

- John Dryden

In the vibrant corridors of St. Paul School, Derapather, a new tradition was about to take root. The virtue Award, a prestigious accolade designed to honor the most virtuous among the teaching staff, was introduced by the school board.

Mrs. Mamoni Saha, a high school teacher known for her patience and wisdom, was the first to receive this honor. Her classroom was an oasis of learning, where respect and kindness were integral as reading and arithmatic.

The day of the award ceremony arrived, and the entire school gathered in the auditorium. The Principal who had the privilage to lead the school took the stage, praising Mrs. Mamoni Saha's nurturing spirit and her ability to see the potential in every child. As she accepted the award, her eyes glistened with humble pride.

This celebration of virtue sparked a ripple effect throughout the remote village of Assam. Teachers strove not just for academic excellence but for moral greatness, and students learned that virtue was the truest measure of success.

While virtue is often its own reward, providing tangible rewards further acknowledges the value of virtuous behavior. Rewards can range from formal recognition and awards to opportunities for personal and professional development.

Establishing an annual "Virtue Award" within an organization to honor employees who exemplify outstanding moral and ethical behavior creates a formal structure for recognizing and rewarding virtue.

Sharing Inspirational Stories

"Virtue has a veil, vice a mask."

- Victor Hugo

"Threads of Kindness" : In the bustling city of Kolkata, where the Howrah Bridge stood as a testament to resilience, there existed a unique partnership—one that transcended classroom walls and touched lives in profound ways.

De Paul Academy, Kolkata nestled amidst the chaotic streets, a group of compassionate teachers and enthusiastic students embarked on a transformative project. Their mission? To bridge the gap between the privileged and the marginalized, weaving threads of kindness that would bind their hearts forever.

The project began with a visit to Cheshire Home-a haven for the destitute, where elderly residents found refuge. The children's eyes widened as they entered the home. The air smelled of antiseptic, and the walls echoed with stories of struggle and survival. Yet, amidst the faded paint and creaking floorboards, there was an undeniable sense of community.

Meet Selina Sebastian, a spirited seventh-grader with a penchant for storytelling and singing. Her eyes sparkled as she listened to Mrs. Das, an elderly resident who had once been a renowned poet. Mrs. Das's hands trembled, but her voice remained steady as she recited verses that had once graced literary magazines. Selina vowed to preserve these words, to honor the legacy of a woman who had fallen through life's cracks.

The teachers played their part too. Mrs. Mou Sengupta, the art teacher, organized weekly workshops. Armed with brushes and colors, the children sat alongside the residents, painting landscapes that captured Kolkata's soul—the Howrah Bridge, the flower markets, and the monsoon-soaked streets. The canvases became a bridge themselves, connecting generations and erasing loneliness.

But it wasn't just about art. Mrs. Biswas, the science teacher, introduced gardening. The children planted marigolds and mint, their small hands digging into the soil alongside those of Mrs. Helen, a retired professor. As the flowers bloomed, so did friendships. Mrs. Helen shared stories of her academic pursuits, and the children listened, wide-eyed, realizing that knowledge was ageless.

The highlight of the project was the "Literary Exchange." The children wrote letters to the residents, sharing their dreams, fears, and favorite books. In return, the residents penned heartfelt replies, their shaky handwriting revealing wisdom forged through hardship. Selina received a letter from **Mrs. Das,** who wrote, "Words are bridges, my young friend. They connect hearts across time." The school organized a grand event—a "Cheshire Carnival." The courtyard buzzed with excitement as stalls sprouted like mushrooms. Selina manned the storytelling booth, narrating Mrs. Das's poems. Mrs. Biswas's art corner displayed vibrant paintings, and Mrs. Gupta's garden yielded fresh mint tea. The residents beamed, their faces lined with gratitude.

As the sun dipped below the horizon, the children and residents gathered around a bonfire. Selina recited a poem she had written—a tribute to Mrs. Das, the bridge-builder. Tears glistened in the old poet's eyes as she whispered, "You've woven my life into your words, my little angel."

And so, the threads of kindness grew stronger. The children visited Cheshire Home regularly, not as volunteers but as friends.

They learned that compassion wasn't a one-time project; it was a lifelong commitment. The teachers, too, discovered that education extended beyond textbooks—it was about nurturing empathy, resilience, and love.

The children of De Paul Academy, who carried the rich experience they had forward like lanterns in the dark. In the quiet corners of Kolkata, where the Howrah Bridge spanned the Hooghly River, the threads of kindness continued to weave lives together. Children, teachers, and the destitute-they had become a family, bound not by pity but by shared humanity.

Sharing the stories of virtuous individuals inspires others to adopt similar values and behaviors. Highlight their actions and the impact they have on their communities through newsletters, social media, or public speaking events.

Encouraging Virtuous Leadership

"Leadership is not about being in charge. It is about taking care of those in your charge."

- Simon Sinek

Virtuous individuals often make excellent leaders due to their commitment to ethical behavior and the well-being of others. Encourage and support their growth into leadership roles where they can influence and inspire broader change.

"Threads of Reverence" :

In the northeastern corner of India, where emerald hills cradle ancient secrets, lies the state of Manipur. Here, the air is thick with devotion, and the land itself breathes stories.

Mount Koubru, known as *Mount Koupalu* in the local tongue, stands tall—a sentinel between earth and sky. Its peaks kiss the heavens, and its slopes cradle legends. For centuries, it has been the abode of gods—the dwelling place of *Lainingthou Koubru* and *Goddess Kounu*. Their presence weaves through the mist, whispering to pilgrims who ascend its rocky paths.

Pangmoul-Motbung, a twin village nestled at the mountain's feet, is a tapestry of resilience. Its people—farmers, weavers, dreamers—live in harmony with the land. The village is a mosaic of terraced fields, where rice sways like golden waves. Here, the Imphal River flows—a silver ribbon connecting past and present.

Arjun, a young farmer from Motbung, gazes at Mount Koubru each morning. His father taught him the ancient hymns—the ones that invoke blessings from the mountain. Arjun knows that the letters of Meetei Mayek, the local script, still exist atop Koubru. They form a cosmic shield, guarding warriors and their dreams.

One monsoon, as rain drummed on tin roofs, Arjun had a vision. He saw the mountain's stone formations, a single face etched in granite. Each crease resembled a Meitei alphabet, the 27 letters that wove their language. Arjun believed that the mountain held the wisdom of ages the whispers of ancestors.

He rallied the villagers. Together, they climbed Mount Koubru, their footsteps echoing ancient hymns. They carried offerings flowers, incense, and hope. At the peak, they stood before the stone-face, their hearts open. Arjun recited the invocation: *"Awang Koubru Asuppa Leima-Lai Khunda Ahanba."*

The mountain listened. The wind carried their prayers across valleys. The Imphal River shimmered below, as if nodding in agreement. The villagers felt the threads of reverence binding them their lives woven into Koubru's legacy.

Word spread. Pilgrims arrived old and young, seeking solace. They touched the stone-formations, tracing the alphabets. Arjun became their guide, sharing stories of virtue, courage, and compassion. The mountain became a bridge a thread connecting hearts.

And so, in the shadow of Mount Koubru, Motbung thrived. The terraced fields yielded abundance, and the Imphal River whispered secrets. Arjun knew that leadership wasn't about titles; it was about service. He became the village head, not by decree but by example.

As the sun dipped behind Koubru, Arjun stood on its slopes. He saw the village below the smoke rising from hearths, the children chasing dragonflies. And he whispered, "Thank you."

For in the state of Manipur, where mountains touch the divine, Arjun had become a bridge builder a thread that bound Koubru, Imphal, and Motbung into a single story of reverence.

Creating Opportunities for Growth

"Virtue is not left to stand alone. He who practices it will have neighbors."

- Confucius

Creating opportunities for personal and professional growth allows virtuous individuals to expand their influence and continue their positive contributions. Provide access to training, mentorship, and development programs that align with their values.

Offering scholarships for further education to students who demonstrate exceptional moral character and community service supports their growth and empowers them to make a greater impact.

Building a Culture of Virtue

"Virtue is the only true nobility."

- Thomas Fuller

Building a culture that values and rewards virtue encourages everyone to strive for moral and ethical excellence. Establish policies and practices that promote transparency, fairness, and integrity across all levels of an organization or community.

Implementing a code of conduct that emphasizes ethical behavior, transparency, and respect for all members sets a clear standard and expectation for virtuous behavior within an organization.

Fostering Virtue Through Mentorship

"Mentoring is a brain to pick, an ear to listen, and a push in the right direction."

- John C. Crosby

Pairing virtuous individuals with mentors who share their values can enhance their development and broaden their impact.

Mentorship provides guidance, support, and opportunities for growth, reinforcing the importance of virtue.

Creating a mentorship program where experienced professionals guide young employees known for their ethical behavior fosters a continuous cycle of virtue and excellence.

Celebrating Virtue in Community Events

"Do not be embarrassed by your failures, learn from them and start again."

- Richard Branson

Celebrating virtuous individuals in community events highlights their contributions and sets an example for others to follow. Organize events that honor those who exemplify virtues like kindness, honesty, and courage.

Hosting a community awards banquet to recognize local heroes who have made significant positive impacts through their virtuous actions brings attention to their efforts and encourages others to emulate their behavior.

Conclusion: Honoring Excellence in Character

Rewarding virtuous people is about more than just recognizing their individual contributions; it's about honoring excellence in character and fostering a culture where virtue is celebrated and encouraged. By recognizing virtue in action, offering praise and gratitude, providing tangible rewards, sharing inspirational stories, encouraging virtuous leadership, creating opportunities for growth, building a culture of virtue, fostering virtue through mentorship, and celebrating virtue in community events, we affirm the importance of moral and ethical behavior in all aspects of life.

In doing so, we create environments where integrity, compassion, and justice are valued and promoted, fostering stronger relationships and more successful communities. Embrace the opportunity to reward virtuous people in your life, and let their example inspire you and others to uphold the highest standards of moral and ethical excellence.

Chapter: 19

In Weaving Lives: Watch, Pray, and Wish Everyone Well

Life presents us with a variety of situations, from joyful to challenging, each requiring a different response. Regardless of the circumstances, adopting a mindset of vigilance, spiritual connection, and goodwill can help us navigate life's complexities with grace and integrity. This chapter explores the principles of watching, praying, and wishing everyone well to guide you in embodying these principles in all aspects of life.

Watch: Stay Vigilant and Observant

"Watch, stand fast in the faith, be brave, be strong." -

1 Corinthians 16:13

Staying vigilant means being aware of your surroundings, understanding the dynamics at play, and recognizing potential challenges and opportunities. Vigilance helps you make informed decisions and respond appropriately to various situations.

Strategies for Staying Vigilant:

1. Stay Informed : Keep yourself updated with relevant information about your environment, whether personal, professional, or social.

Regularly reading reputable news sources helps you stay informed about current events and developments that may affect you.

2. Practice Mindfulness : Engage in mindfulness practices to stay present and aware of your thoughts, feelings, and surroundings.

Daily meditation or mindfulness exercises can help you develop a keen sense of awareness and focus.

3. Reflect and Assess : Regularly reflect on your experiences and assess your actions to learn and grow.

Keeping a journal where you note daily observations and reflections can help you identify patterns and areas for improvement.

Pray: Seek Spiritual Connection and Guidance

"Prayer is not asking. It is a longing of the soul. It is daily admission of one's weakness. It is better in prayer to have a heart without words than words without a heart." - Mahatma Gandhi

Prayer, in its many forms, allows you to connect with your spiritual beliefs, seek guidance, and find peace amidst life's challenges. It provides a sense of comfort and purpose, helping you navigate difficult times with resilience and hope.

Strategies for Cultivating a Prayerful Life:

1. Daily Prayer : Establish a routine of daily prayer or spiritual practice that aligns with your beliefs.

Set aside a few minutes each morning or evening for prayer or meditation to center yourself and seek guidance.

2. Community Worship : Participate in community worship or spiritual gatherings to strengthen your faith and find support.

Joining a local church, mosque, temple, or meditation group can provide a sense of community and shared purpose.

3. Express Gratitude : Incorporate gratitude into your prayers, acknowledging the positive aspects of your life and expressing thanks.

Start or end your prayers with a moment of gratitude, focusing on the blessings and positive experiences in your life.

Wish Everyone Well: Foster Goodwill and Compassion

"Do unto others as you would have them do unto you."

- The Golden Rule

Wishing everyone well, regardless of their actions or attitudes, cultivates an environment of compassion and empathy. It helps you maintain a positive outlook and fosters healthy relationships and communities.

Strategies for Wishing Everyone Well:

1. Practice Empathy : Try to understand others' perspectives and experiences, even when they differ from your own.

In a conflict situation, take a moment to consider the other person's feelings and motivations before responding.

2. Offer Kindness : Extend acts of kindness and support to those around you, regardless of their behavior toward you.

A simple act of kindness, like holding the door open for someone or offering a smile, can brighten someone's day and promote goodwill.

3. Release Resentment : Let go of grudges and resentment, recognizing that holding onto negative emotions only harms you.

Practice forgiveness, not necessarily for others, but to free yourself from the burden of anger and bitterness.

Real-Life Application: Balancing Vigilance, Prayer, and Goodwill

In the Workplace

- **Watch:** Stay vigilant by keeping up with industry trends and understanding your company's dynamics.
- **Pray:** Seek guidance and strength through prayer or meditation before important meetings or decisions.
- **Wish Everyone Well** : Foster a positive work environment by supporting colleagues and wishing them success, even in competitive settings.

In Personal Relationships

- **Watch:** Be attentive to the needs and emotions of your loved ones.
- **Pray :** Pray for the well-being and happiness of your family and friends.
- **Wish Everyone Well** : Extend compassion and forgiveness in conflicts, aiming to maintain harmony and understanding.

In Community Involvement

- **Watch:** Stay informed about community issues and needs.
- **Pray :** Seek spiritual support for your community's well-being.
- **Wish Everyone Well :** Engage in volunteer work and support initiatives that promote the common good.

Conclusion:

Living with Awareness, Spiritual Connection, and Goodwill

In all situations, adopting the principles of watching, praying, and wishing everyone well helps you navigate life's challenges with resilience, compassion, and integrity. By staying vigilant, seeking spiritual connection, and fostering goodwill, you create a positive environment for yourself and those around you. Embrace these principles as guiding lights in your life, and let them inspire you to live with awareness, empathy, and a steadfast commitment to the well-being of all.

www.ingramcontent.com/pod-product-compliance
Lightning Source LLC
LaVergne TN
LVHW061611070526
838199LV00078B/7248